DEBT AND DANGER

DEBT AND DANGER

The World Financial Crisis

by HAROLD LEVER
and CHRISTOPHER HUHNE

The Atlantic Monthly Press

BOSTON / NEW YORK

FIRST AMERICAN EDITION

LIBRARY OF CONGRESS CATALOG CARD NUMBER 86-70573

BP

PRINTED IN THE UNITED STATES OF AMERICA

FOR
DIANE AND VICKY

CONTENTS

Debt and Danger is about the international debt crisis which affects everyone. Certainly no American community is secure from the disaster which would follow any significant default on their dollar obligations by countries in Latin America, Africa and Asia. Debt needs our urgent attention for the threat it poses in itself – but also because it epitomises a sickness in the West. It is a dramatic crystallisation of the failure of Western democracies during the last twenty years to adapt to a new world of economic interdependence so that now in the mid-1980s we have, as well as a crisis of debt, a dangerous volatility in our exchange rates and a growing menace to free trade.

The Western countries co-operated brilliantly after the devastation of World War II, and there was a unique advance in the creation of wealth. The co-operation lasted a generation. But the succeeding generation did not build on the post-war achievements. When we needed to adapt our collective institutions to meet the complexities of the 1970s and 1980s, we failed. Collective effort came to be made only ad hoc and only when reality broke so decisively into insularity that even the zealots of benign neglect were shamed into temporary silence. The six or seven major countries and the smaller ones which make up the West drifted off into a form of economic isolationism. They sought to manage their economies more or less as if they were separate entities. It was an illusion and the crack in the facade is now plain to see.

This is a regression to the mentality which prevailed after 1918. Economies then, as today, operated on national impulses with only intermittent recognition that individual achievement is related to global success. We know what happened: the depression and Hitler. The experience taught our leaders that prosperity for individual countries could be achieved only if, in certain key areas, bridges were built between them. The grave danger to the common good of individual protectionism was acknowledged in the General Agreement on Trade and Tariffs (GATT) and the commitment made to freer trade. The enormous cost of competitive devaluation and beggar-my-neighbor policies which had scarred the 1930s was recognised and dealt with in the Bretton Woods system of fixed exchange rates and the creation of the International Monetary Fund to provide even-handed support in periods of balance-of-payments adjustments. Those bridges represented a new maturity. The leaders of the world, it could be claimed, had at last come to recognise that world prosperity could be achieved only by world co-operation.

The subsequent forty years have shown this judgement to be too hasty. True, we created institutions, but we built them more in the spirit of completing a task of organisation than of dedicating ourselves to a principle. Looking back, it seems that what was achieved depended too little on a shared and settled wisdom and too much on US leadership. The dominance of the United States could not survive the recovery in Europe and Japan. The recovery was largely due to the years of co-operation, and it ought logically to have converted a practice into a confirmed custom. That it did not can only be due to the underlying fragility of purpose. As US predominance was reduced, other countries, particularly in Europe, were increasingly disinclined to play within the spirit of the new rules. Nationalism, parochialism and sectionalism overtook co-operation. The same blight began to affect other countries, including the United States itself. The regression has been very clear for many years in trade, exchange-rate (parity) management and adjustment to trade deficits. Dire results have followed. The ramshackle arrangements in the area of sovereign borrowing which have led inevitably to the debt crisis are another child of the regression.

In this new world of dispersed power, no country has been sure of its roles and responsibilities. Most critically this has been true of the United States. In the retreat from co-operation to insularity over the last twenty years, the United States has been unable to exert consistent leadership. No longer able to impose its will through power, great though this is, it has not developed an alternative style of leadership based on reason and enlightened self-interest.

This may now be changing. There is at least hope in the spectacle of two very intelligent somersaults. The first is on currency. After years of laissez-faire, the Secretary of the US

Treasury, Mr James Baker, induced the finance ministers of the leading five countries to strive for a realignment of currencies and to diminish the gross distortion of the dollar. The principal stimulus seems not to have been a flash of insight about the principle of co-operation, but the fear of the world's authorities that protectionism in the United States was about to become uncontrollable. The co-operation among the five worked to the extent that it corrected the gross distortion of the dollar. And it certainly signalled some perception that unmanaged floating is no longer tolerable. Unfortunately, there is little sign that the cause of the distortion of parities has been understood. There has not been a strategic review of the principles which should now determine parity levels. The systemic weaknesses remain, and in the absence of a commitment to collective response which is defined and sustained, there will be another gross deformity before long.

The second somersault is over the debt crisis. Secretary Baker has again taken a lead, seeking new commitments from the banks and the International Monetary Fund. The proposed operation is far too small in scale and too impromptu – as will be apparent, we trust, in the course of this book – but it is the first serious recognition by a powerful politician of the dangers which beset us. It could open the way to a new era of co-operation. Much depends on the responses of the Europeans and Japanese.

There is an echo here of the Marshall Plan. It was an American initiative which transformed Europe from a war-shattered wreck to an engine for world recovery. But the Marshall Plan was not a set of blueprints, released one day from Washington. The original US thoughts in the Marshall Plan were more vague and tentative than those of Secretary Baker in the debt crisis. What turned the thoughts into a real plan for execution, with immense benefit to the United States as well as Europe, was the prompt response from the Europeans at the highest level. Though the British Treasury played its part in financial detail, the inspiration for the UK response came from Prime Minister Clement Attlee and Foreign Secretary Ernest Bevin. They at once recognised the immense political potential.

The responsibilities then required from Europe were not great and the rewards were obvious and immediate. Can today's leaders of Europe and Japan show as much imaginative resolve?

The benefits, although real, are not so obvious. There does not seem to have been a proper appreciation that, because most of the lending is dollar lending, the great banks outside the United States are even more perilously exposed than those within the United States. Their central banks do not have the necessary dollars to act as lender of last resort. An effective response from Europe and Japan to the US initiatives is therefore crucial for resolving the debt problem – and for achieving greater currency stability.

On debt, they must sit down with the United States and put flesh on the Baker plan. They must make it effective and take their share of the cost of supporting it. On the currency question, they must join with the United States in agreeing on systems to maintain stability when the dollar's parity is brought to a point compatible with an acceptable world balance. And they must take into account that domestic economic policies, especially interest-rate policies, will need to be adjusted accordingly.

The path we are advocating will not be easy. At present no government or parliament has adequate mechanisms for analysing economic policy as a whole to achieve the right blend between international and domestic considerations. The unresolved problem of the US trade deficit, for example, hangs like a black cloud over the world economy. Japanese, European and South American economies have become heavily dependent on this imbalance in the US economy which must before long be cured. It used to be said that when America caught a cold the rest of the world got pneumonia. The way things are going, when America gets well the rest of the world will catch influenza.

There are many more lethal viruses in the fantasy that nations can continue to go it alone. The time may not yet be ripe for a grand plan to reproduce the efforts at the end of the war. But perhaps our leaders can now recognise that this is what is needed and that they have a chance of achieving it. In this sense the present dangers may be therapeutic. They concentrate minds, obviously; but they must also elevate them.

February 1986

DEBT AND DANGER

INTRODUCTION AND SUMMARY

We have made a labyrinth and have got lost
in it. We must find our way again.

DENIS DIDEROT

The flows of finance between the advanced and the developing worlds, which have in the past done so much to promote economic stability, employment and the progress of living standards, are now characterized by a perverse and dangerous anomaly. Until 1982 it was understood that there had to be, for a prolonged period, a one-way flow of resources from the advanced countries to the Third World to promote its development. The view went unchallenged in either official or private-sector circles and was supported by every school of economic thought, albeit for differing reasons. Since the debt crisis which broke in 1982, those flows have been reversed for each important group of countries in the Third World. International Monetary Fund (IMF) estimates imply that in 1985 there is to be a resource flow from the seven largest Third World borrowers to their more prosperous creditors worth $32 billion, or nearly one-fifth of their entire earnings from the sales of their exports of goods and services.[1]

This reverse or negative flow is a perversion of common sense and of sound economics. On a classical view, the developing countries should attract capital from the industrial world because they are able to increase output by more than rich countries for a given increase in investment. On an alternative view, the debtors need balance-of-payments finance because their domestic economies are capable of expanding more rapidly than they are able to increase their foreign-exchange earnings and imports, due mainly to their reliance on export commodities whose demand grows less rapidly than world income. To our knowledge, no economist has yet advocated a large flow of resources from the poorer countries as a way of stimulating their economic progress.

Nor was this ever the intention of those who encouraged or undertook the original lending to the debtors, the interest payments on which are the main cause of the reverse transfer. It was always implicitly assumed that the financial markets would continue to refinance old debt and extend new credit so that the flow of resources to the developing world would continue, at least until some far-distant future in which the debtors would reach a level of development where it was feasible and desirable for them to export rather than import capital. This unplanned reverse flow of resources is made all the more extraordinary because it has been elevated into a necessary symptom of 'adjustment' by the official policy of the industrial countries, which are as unwilling today to take their proper responsibility for the healthy functioning of the world's economy as they were after the first oil shock of 1973, which laid the foundations for this anomaly.

Yet such abdication of responsibility is singularly misplaced. The world's financial safety and economic health is balanced on a knife-edge. If defaults halt the reverse flows, many of the largest banks in the advanced countries will become insolvent. A crisis of the kind which we have thankfully not experienced since the Great Crash of 1929 would once again be a terrible reality. But if the Third World's debtors continue to generate the large trade surpluses required to make payment to the advanced countries, their economic development, already manifestly inadequate, will be hobbled for a generation. The effort to sustain the large trade surpluses required imposes enormous strains on the world's trading system, as industries in the advanced countries have to make way for Third World exports and resist the adjustment by means of ever more strident appeals for protectionism. Moreover, the very uncertainty of continued payments in these circumstances of rising political pressures in both debtor and creditor countries causes the banks themselves to slow down their lending, adding a further depressive influence to world trade.

The debtors can do no more to resolve their predicament. All the pressures on them are to expand their economies more rapidly, which would inevitably entail smaller rather than larger trading surpluses and would quite possibly result in creeping defaults on debt. The bankers cannot realistically lend more money to offset the interest payments coming back to them on the outstanding debt without a further loss of credibility. As it is, their outstanding lending to the Third World outstrips their own capital by a factor of two or more. Only the governments and monetary authorities of the advanced countries have the resources and the standing to reconcile the interests of both debtors and bankers – and to safeguard the world economy.

It is not, though, their unique financial power which alone casts the advanced-country governments in the natural role of managers of the debt crisis. They also bear a heavy responsibility for the events which led up to its occurrence. Until 1973 it was widely understood that commercial lending was not a safe or sure vehicle for development finance. Banks could neither impose conditions to ensure the fruitful use of the funds they lent, nor could they, when the need arose, postpone debt servicing and provide new funds without undermining the confidence of those who deposit money with them. After 1973 it was absolutely right for the advanced countries to seek to ensure that the developing world had the funds to continue to import the material they needed for development, despite the sharp rise in the price of oil. Without those funds, Third World imports would have collapsed and, with them, the jobs of millions in the advanced countries who sell to them. What was wrong was for the advanced-country governments to push the commercial banking systems of their countries into a role which should have been supported and regulated by the authorities whose public purposes it rightly fulfilled.

In the years after the first oil crisis of 1973–4 the banks took the unspent cash surpluses of the oil-rich countries and lent them to the oil-dependent Third World. Reinforced by the approval and encouragement of their governments, the banks happily developed the conviction that there was no risk in this lending to foreign governments. They came to believe that they had hit upon the most profitable area in banking history. Nowhere else could such huge sums be placed at an assured profit and with minimal administrative cost. The banks that lent in this field soon found that the profits from what they had convinced themselves was risk-free lending greatly exceeded those from the rest of their much more complicated and onerous activities.

In the years after 1974 the borrowing countries financed the trade deficits of their imports over their exports increasingly by borrowing from the banks. The borrowing was originally prompted by the need to cover the cartel's oil price rises. It was soon much extended to cover virtually any borrowing that the developing countries' governments saw fit to make. Indeed, countries like Mexico, Venezuela and Nigeria, which were beneficiaries of the oil price rises, were among the heaviest borrowers. There was no thought of servicing the debt by generating trade surpluses and reverse transfers. The service of interest and repayments was expected to be met, and was in fact met year after year, by new borrowing in addition to loans to cover current needs.

The happy-go-lucky assumption by governments and banks that the debts could be serviced indefinitely by new borrowing on the financial markets went virtually unchallenged. All the agreements with debtor countries for service of interest and capital were manifestly on terms which could not be met by the debtors' export earnings but only by new borrowing, as one of the present authors repeatedly warned both within the government between 1974 and 1979 and thereafter.

Yet uncritical self-congratulation over the advantages of these arrangements was the order of the day. The bankers liked them because apparently never were propriety and profit so happily conjoined. The borrowers liked them because they placed little restraint on the volume or the purposes of their borrowing. The Organization of Petroleum Exporting Countries (OPEC) liked them because they enlisted the banking system of the West in support of the ability of their poorest customers to meet the cartel's oil price rises. The aid lobby liked them because they provided a novel transfer of resources to the poorer countries on a scale greater than ever before. Santa Claus had appeared in the guise of sound commercial activity, and nobody wanted to shoot him. Western governments liked these arrangements because they appeared to support their belief that this lending was urgently needed in the world interest and could be dealt with indefinitely by unassisted bank intermediation rather than by recourse to public budgets.

The inexorable result, however, was the crisis of debt and growth which we suffer today. The period between borrowing and servicing of debt by a real flow of foreign currency back to the lender can be bridged by further commercial borrowing – but only as long as that real flow is a credible prospect. Nobody could claim that this prospect grew to match the ever-growing mountain of private debt, and this was bound to bring into question the credibility of most of the debtors and of the lending system itself. The build-up to crisis was inevitable. Prolonged recession and the move to higher real interest rates after 1979 speeded up the disintegration of confidence, but they were not its fundamental cause.

The plan of this book is as follows. In Chapter 2 we deal in greater depth with the mounting total of debt, show its heavy concentration among a handful of leading debtor countries, especially in Latin America, and among the leading banks of the advanced countries, and explain the interdependence of the world banking system. We outline the fragility of large banks whose Third World lending substantially exceeds their capital and reserves and show why there is no room for official complacency. The pyramid of debt has proved sustainable since the Mexican crisis of 1982 only because of extraordinary sacrifices on the part of the debtors and considerable effort by creditors and official institutions alike. But most of the factors which have encouraged a 'co-operative' handling of the debt crisis will be hard to sustain.

Reschedulings, whereby certain interest and principal re-payments which come due are postponed when the banks put up some new lending partially to offset them, will become more and more difficult. As it is, the banks are increasing their outstand-ing loans to most of the debtors only under official duress. The structure of the banking market is such that each creditor has an individual interest in reducing its exposure to the debtor coun-tries, though if all creditors followed their individual interest and reduced their exposure (and hence met even fewer of the interest and principal payments coming back to them), the debtor countries would be put in an impossible position very rapidly.

Even if such a crisis could be averted, the situation from the point of view of the debtors looks no happier. Negative transfers and their associated trade surpluses are enormous and growing, despite some new bank lending and funds from the IMF. They have been achieved largely by drastic cuts in imports engineered by a depression of demand, output and employment. The recent increases in exports from the debtor countries, which alleviate the import-cutting effects of the negative transfers, are never-theless woefully dependent on the buoyancy of the American marketplace. That cannot be sustained as American growth slows down and the United States' trade deficit is reduced.

Moreover, several of the reasons why the debtors have so far been prepared to accept the enormous sacrifices demanded of them, rather than to default on their obligations in the face of domestic pressures, may also be waning. The threat of vanishing trade credit if a country defaults is less potent when foreign-exchange reserves are building up and barter trade is growing. They have also hoped that eventually Western governments will come to see the difficulty of their situation and intervene with debt relief. If that prospect is not kept alive, defaults could follow swiftly.

In Chapter 3 we turn to the origins of the crisis and look at the reasons why countries incurred debt. Money – and particularly foreign exchange – is 'fungible' in the sense that it is not always easy to track down its true end use because a loan can easily be transferred to purposes other than those for which it was contracted. Lending is thus general lending to the country concerned to maintain a higher level of imports than would otherwise be the case and in the hope that it will be able to repay. With these caveats, it is clear that the increased oil bill of the non-oil Third World countries was the main cause of the debt build-up from the debtors' point of view, though rising interest rates and mistaken exchange-rate policies also played a role.

For every borrower, however, there is a lender. In Chapter 4 we look at the origins of the crisis from the point of view of the suppliers of credit, particularly noting the mechanisms in the Euro-market which allowed the banks to believe that the lending was sounder than it turned out to be. We also deal with some of the arguments of the leading banking advocates of the lending, notably the former head of Citibank, Mr Walter Wriston, and explain the fallacies behind the belief that sovereign borrowers are particularly safe risks. However, we also quote chapter and verse from various instances of official encouragement of the lending and describe the way in which Western governments ran away from the problems their policies helped to create.

In Chapter 5 we turn to an analysis of how the advanced countries, through their combined monetary institution the IMF, now foresee that the crisis will be resolved. We explain in detail why there is a conflict of interest between the banks' attempt to protect their fragile balance sheets by restricting their lending and the debtors' need for foreign exchange if they are to grow. In drawing out the implications of the IMF's baseline scenario, we show that the rates of growth which it projects for the developing country debtors – if they hold to the prescribed course of generating large reverse transfers – are far from satisfactory in terms of either living standards or unemployment. We also show that, despite these disappointing growth rates, the IMF expects these countries to go on generating enormous (and in some cases growing) negative transfers in order to meet their obligations, a prospect which is wholly implausible.

The surprise is, however, that even if the debtor countries hold to the IMF's scenario and do not succumb to the temptation to grow more quickly (and import more), the position of the banks will hardly have improved by the end of the decade. The world's major financial institutions will remain, on realistic assumptions about the likely growth of their capital base, as vulnerable to default as they are today. Nor are there any easy ways of resolving the banker–debtor dilemma through an increase in other types of private finance to the developing world, for the increases required in, say, bond finance or private direct investment would be so enormous as to be incredible.

In Chapter 6 we examine some of the IMF's and others' assumptions about world growth and other macro-economic conditions and find that there is no likely (or unlikely) change in world circumstances which will relieve policy-makers of the need to tackle the debt problem. A sharp fall in oil prices now, for example, would merely aggravate the debt problems of oil-exporting countries like Mexico without providing enough help to oil importers like Brazil. The projected scale of negative transfers is simply too large to be reversed easily by a fall in interest rates or a decline in the dollar. However, there are substantial downside risks in the present situation which could make the debt problem worse, notably the evidence of a steady increase in protectionism against the exports of the developing world. The advanced countries are doing much to frustrate the Third World's attempts to repay its debt in the only way it can – by increasing its trade surpluses and its exports. Ominously, this was one of the causes of the chain of defaults during the 1930s.

In Chapter 7 we turn to the predicament of some leading South American debtors and examine the political pressures which are pushing them towards a unilateral limit on debt service, or creeping default. Their overall level of income is low and maldistributed. Social unrest is mounting. The new urban working class has expressed its discontent through labour militancy and sporadic outbreaks of rioting and looting. The middle class, whose expectations rose markedly in the years of high growth, have seen the prospect of consolidating their gains crumble. Against a background of the increasing political appeals for moratoria and debt-service restrictions, we look at the implications of several individual forecasts of the outlook for Argentina, Mexico and Brazil, the three largest Latin American debtors. The negative transfers expected of these countries are utterly far-fetched, and the sanctions which some claim might be imposed against a defaulter are a mirage. A default in these crucial countries cannot be ruled out on either economic or political grounds.

In Chapter 8 we sketch out the likely consequences of defaults for the world financial system and the world economy. Few of the more exposed banks could escape effective nationalization. A bank which found so much of its loans of no value would also have to cut back on other loans by a multiple of the original default, so that a sharp recession would ensue. There would be gravely disruptive consequences for the whole world's banking system. The advanced countries would pay many times over any costs of a modest reform of present arrangements. In the second part of the chapter we argue that the present situation not only entails the risk of a crash but also exacts continuing costs from both debtors and creditors even while a collapse is averted.

This paradox, whereby the repayment of debt makes the creditor countries poorer rather than richer, arises from the nature of the world economy, whose activity is not a zero-sum game. One participant's success does not imply another's failure. All can lose, or all can gain. The attempt of the debtors to repay their obligations by cutting their imports and generating more exports increases unemployment in the rich countries and ensures a deflationary bias to the world economy. The profligate, unregulated lending of 1973–82 greatly advantaged the world, even if the whole of the lending were ultimately to be defaulted. But the mirror-image paradox is that the present repayment of that debt is disadvantaging both debtors and creditors.

In Chapter 9 we draw the strands of the argument together and set out some criteria for a solution to the debt problem. We look briefly at some of the proposals which have been put forward and explain what their failings are. Finally, we set out our own preferred proposals for dealing with the crisis. Regulated, official guarantees for commercial bank lending to the debtor countries would help to resolve both aspects of the debt problem. They would be adequate at least to ensure that the reverse transfers were ended and that debtor growth and imports could resume a normal path. They would thus also implicitly guarantee the worth of the outstanding debt of these countries and hence the health of the banks. Such a programme would give the banks time to make appropriate write-offs of the existing debt and hence limit the need for guaranteed lending to pay the interest on the debt overhang.

Whatever optimism governments choose to nourish about the far-distant future, they must now concede that there is no prospect of full service of these banks' debts either by the countries concerned or by refinance in the markets in the years immediately ahead. This means policy will continue to be dependent on rescheduling, the credibility of which is fast running out and, with it, confidence in the stability of our leading banks. The markets' refusal to find further finance for the debtors calls into question not only the debtors' solvency but, by ominous implication, the solvency of their creditors too. In the years ahead, therefore, with existing policies we will, even on the most hopeful view, be continuously at risk from widespread default and its calamitous consequences. The world cannot prosper with a banking system whose solvency is chronically dependent on unsupported optimism about future debt payments and with South American and other developing economies struggling with grim economic and political difficulties.

The moves in the summer of 1985 to limit debt servicing by Peru and South Africa underline the urgency of the problem. Above all, there must be protection against the most immediate perils of major defaults by the debtors to the banks. The bank debts are a hangover from the emergency responses to the oil shocks and ill-thought-out methods for recycling the OPEC money. But vital world purposes were served, however clumsily. It is not in the interests of our peoples to have governments encourage and approve these bank commitments and then walk away to leave the banking system and the debtors to financial collapse. Most of the populist clamour against 'bailing out the banks' is based on ignorance of the history of this lending and of the consequences of its breakdown. The failure of governments so far to acknowledge their responsibility has been due not to moral principle but to political timidity.

The official response to present difficulties is as little thought out and as much under the pressure of immediate concerns as the reactions of 1974. The problem is not to discover a solution which will protect the major interests at risk. We are not immodest enough to suppose that there is any shortage of valid solutions. The difficulty is to get congresses, parliaments and governments to understand the problem, to assess the costs and dangers and to develop the political courage to act. It is to that task that this book is primarily directed.

2

THE STATE OF THE PROBLEM

Hope is a good breakfast but a bad supper.
FRANCIS BACON

In the financial and economic worlds events rarely reach some climactic turning-point which an observer can say firmly divides innocence from experience. The Wall Street crash of 1929 was preceded by years of hectic speculation and followed by a protracted downwards spiral of credit, trade, output and employment which was to continue in most countries until 1931. The world debt crisis which resulted was a child of the crash and the depression, but its consequences came in instalments for many years afterwards, gradually and agonizingly writing down the foreign bonds which European and American investors bought in the full expectation that their savings would be secure.[1] It was not until 1931, two years after the first downturn of financial prices and world activity, that the telegrams from the finance ministries of the debtor countries of the day began to land on desks in New York and London announcing their inability temporarily to service their external debts.

Protracted negotiations with the representatives of bondholders – the 1930s equivalent of the rescheduling of payments due in the 1980s to the Western banks – kept alive the hope of full payment. Not until September of 1933, when the world economy was picking itself up from the catastrophe of 1929–31, did Mexico's President Rodriguez declare that the present and future financial policy of his government did not admit of renewing service on the foreign debt. In Brazil it was 1937 before the unilateral suspension of all debt servicing was announced. In Argentina, the Roca–Runciman treaties, which guaranteed sterling bond-holders a preference in foreign exchange, were finally overturned with the nationalist-populist coup of 1943. These slowly unfolding events of the 1930s could only too easily find a parallel today.

The world debt crisis of the 1980s is similar in many respects. The greatest debtors of today are the countries which defaulted in the 1930s and, in many cases, repeatedly throughout the nineteenth century. Their predicament today is also similar: they are relatively poor countries, in the grip of economic forces outside their control, attempting to reconcile the social and political imperative of growth with the claims of the Western financial system.

The difference today is that a handful of these countries – notably the largest debtors in Latin America – have the power to inflict grave damage on some of the world's largest banks. In the 1930s a default on bonds which reduced them to a fraction of their face value was a personal calamity for many thousands of European and American investors, but it did not undermine the integrity of the financial system. Today a unilateral and long-standing default by Mexico, Brazil, Argentina and Venezuela could wipe out the capital of seven of the nine largest banks in the United States and two of the four in Britain, with consequential damage to the entire banking system. The outcome would involve governments in taking over, running and managing a large tranche of their banking systems, however distasteful that might prove to ministerial prejudices. There would inevitably be a process of credit contraction, which would leave few companies untouched. As the banks called in their loans, so businesses would scramble to realize their cash, meeting the demand for their products from their stocks and saving money by cutting output and employment.

The world debt crisis is far from over, however hopeful may be the past tenses sometimes employed by bankers and finance ministers when they refer to it. In reality, few of the characteristics of the financial structure have changed since 1982 in a way which can be said to have made it less fragile; the essential co-operation between world monetary authorities, the debtor countries and private creditor banks remains precarious. Their mutual dependence is as great as ever, and their safety is unsupported by any coherent, agreed framework. If the banks collapsed, their depositors and shareholders would suffer major losses except to the extent that governments were able and willing to mitigate the consequences.

Estimates of the amount of developing-country debt vary slightly from source to source, due mainly to small differences in definition and method. But on one fact all the bodies which produce official estimates – the IMF, the World Bank, the

Organization for Economic Co-operation and Development (OECD) and the Bank for International Settlements (BIS) – are agreed: the total went on rising in 1984. On the World Bank's estimates, the liabilities of the developing countries rose by a further $52 billion to reach $895 billion in 1984.[2] Of this total, $142 billion was short-term debt with a maturity, when it was issued, of less than one year: a category of finance extended overwhelmingly to fund trade and mainly by private commercial banks. In addition, some $472 billion of long-term debt was also from private sources. A second inconvenient fact is that this debt, and particularly private debt, is concentrated among relatively few of the developing countries. On the IMF's estimates, just thirty-three countries in the western hemisphere – in Latin America and the Caribbean – accounted for 42 per cent of the total debt of all 123 indebted developing countries in 1984.[3] Just seven major borrowers – Argentina, Mexico, Brazil, Venezuela, South Korea, Indonesia and the Philippines – accounted for 44 per cent, the vast majority of it commercial debt to private banks (see Table 1).

Table 1   The foreign-currency bank debt of the seven biggest developing-country debtors, March 1985 ($ million)

Brazil	76,744
Mexico	72,115
South Korea	31,211
Argentina	26,226
Venezuela	25,180
Indonesia	14,338
Philippines	13,319
Total	259,133
(Implied IMF total, 1984	360,000)[1]

Note: [1] The BIS's estimates probably under-record bank debt by excluding some borrowing from offshore financial centres. They also exclude loans from official lenders like the IMF and the World Bank. The implied IMF total for these seven countries is derived from IMF, *World Economic Outlook*, Washington DC, April 1985, which gives figures for the debt–export ratio of the group and for its exports.

Source: BIS, *International Banking Developments, First Quarter 1985*, Basle, July 1985, Table 5.

This is not to argue that the burden of debt is negligible in other parts of the world. Clearly, the poorest countries in Africa and Asia would be in a less parlous state if the burden of their debt were lifted. In sub-Saharan Africa, in particular, there is a human and economic crisis of terrible proportions. The urgent case for fresh resources to stave off famine is unanswerable in moral terms. However, the problems of these countries are not the central concern of this book, since the danger of present financial arrangements for the world as a whole lies in the interdependence of the big borrowing countries and the commercial banks which lend to them. The overwhelming bulk of the debt finance for the low-income countries has come from governments and multilateral institutions like the World Bank instead of the commercial banks. Unlike banks, official lenders are able to roll over loans in times of need without endangering their own financial safety. Moreover, they have accepted for the most part a fixed and often subsidized interest rate on the lending, so that interest payments, as a proportion of exports for the low-income countries, rose modestly from 4.7 per cent in 1977 to 5.4 per cent in 1983.[4] By contrast, the rise in interest payments for the big borrowers of South America was from 10 per cent of exports to 32 per cent. The debt crisis *per se* is a problem of big-borrowing countries; it is also, as we shall see, a problem of big banks – and, indeed, of the world banking system.

The banks like to point out that their lending to developing countries is a small proportion of what they call their 'total assets' – their lending and other money owed to them in the form, say, of short-term government bills. But this is not a relevant figure: total assets for a bank are stated before deducting what is owed to their depositors and other creditors. Using this approach, a man who had £1 million worth of assets but also owed £1 million could claim to own £1 million worth of assets. His net worth, however, would be zero. Moreover, he could still claim he had £1 million worth of assets even if they turned out to be worth less than the £1 million he had expected. He is entitled under law to call an asset good until it is recognized as defective. If debts go sour, it is the banks' own capital, reserves or profits which alone can meet the loss. When these are not enough, and banks have to use other people's money, they are no longer solvent. Indeed, even the threat of serious depletion of a bank's own assets always triggers a run on the bank by anxious depositors.

As a proportion of the banks' own capital and reserves, their loans to the developing countries are very large indeed. Not surprisingly, the United States banks are the largest lenders to the developing world. The 209 American banking organizations which report to the Federal Financial Institutions Examination Council had $132.6 billion outstanding in loans to the Third World (including OPEC countries such as Nigeria and Venezuela) in June 1984, while their capital amounted to $85 billion.[5] In other words, this lending amounted to 156 per cent of their total capital.

The problem for the American banks, though, is not shared equally. The vast majority of small regional banks, themselves the product of the USA's historical insistence on banks taking deposits in only one state, have lent little abroad. That role fell during the 1970s to large banks which have traditionally gathered much of their money on the wholesale or 'inter-bank' market in deposits rather than directly from depositors in the high street. A small high street bank, say, with a surplus of deposits over its own loans lends the excess to bigger banks. Just twenty-four American banks account for 63 per cent of all the reporting banks' assets, but, even more crucially, they account for 78 per cent of all loans to foreigners and 84 per cent of all loans to the Third World – $110.7 billion out of the $132.6 billion total.

The concentration of risk does not end there, for out of those twenty-four banks only nine stand head and shoulders above the rest both in their overall size and in their exposure to foreign risk. These nine 'money-centre' banks – so-called because they are based mainly in New York and deal overwhelmingly in wholesale deposits – account for 43 per cent of all reporting banks' assets, 59 per cent of foreign loans and 63 per cent of all American bank loans to the Third World. There is another source of weakness: these nine banks – Bank of America, Citibank, Chemical, Chase Manhattan, Morgan Guaranty Trust, Manufacturers Hanover, Continental Illinois, Bankers Trust and First National Bank of Chicago – have prided themselves on their need to have only relatively low amounts of their own capital compared with their total loans (or assets) on the grounds that their size enables economies of scale to be made when dealing with risk. A big share of Third World loans and a relatively small amount of capital mean that the nine money centres had on their books Third World debt worth 246 per cent of primary capital. (Primary capital is the American equivalent of a bank's own assets and reserves.)

Figure 1   U S bank claims on non-oil-exporting less developed countries (including Mexico) as a percentage of capital

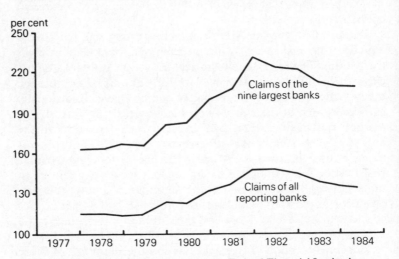

Source: Country Exposure Lending Surveys, Federal Financial Institutions Examination Council.

Figure 1 shows the exposures of both the nine money-centre banks and all the American reporting banks to a sub-category of Third World debtors – the non-oil exporters, including Mexico – as a percentage of the banks' capital. Although this ratio has declined gently from its peak in 1981, the decline is less significant than the degree of exposure. Even if the ratio were to fall sharply in the years ahead, which is unlikely, these banks will continue to be vulnerable to the destruction of their capital by defaults. Moreover, as we argue in Chapter 5, the quality of the capital which has been responsible for the slight fall in the ratio may leave something to be desired.

If anything is certain, of course, it is that the entire Third World, or even a large part of it, is not about to default on its debt. Many countries in Asia can still reasonably be characterized as 'good risks', even if their debt is high. South Korea, for example, is one of the seven biggest Third World debtors, but its strong growth and creditable export performance make it a less likely candidate for crisis. The same, though, cannot be said for many of the other major debtors, and particularly the debtors of Latin America. This region alone accounts for more than 60 per cent of all the money which the nine money-centre banks have lent to the Third World and alone amounts to more than 154 per cent of these banks' primary capital. Four countries alone – Mexico, Brazil, Argentina and Venezuela – had outstanding debt to the nine American money centre banks worth $43.2 billion, or 127 per cent of their capital in June 1984.[6]

Nor is this concentration both of banks and of risk confined to the US financial institutions. For many years the conventional wisdom in the City of London was that Third World and Latin American debt was an American problem. The figures are still scarce, but City of London estimates for the end of 1984 show that Britain's four largest clearing banks – National Westminster, Barclays, Lloyds and the Midland – had loan exposures to Mexico, Brazil, Argentina and Venezuela which match the exposures of the USA's big twenty-four. On American definitions of asset-to-capital ratios, both Lloyds (with 165 per cent of its capital) and the Midland (with 205 per cent) ranked alongside the most exposed of the American money centres. Table 2 shows the exposure of the biggest British and American banks to the biggest Latin American debtors as a percentage of bank capital.

There is a further unpleasant twist to this international exposure. The British, German, French, Italian and other banks' foreign lending is largely in dollars. Their own capital, however, is overwhelmingly in their national currencies. Their lending has mainly been financed, therefore, by dollar deposits. If depositor nervousness brings about their recall, these banks and the respective central banks have very limited dollar resources

Table 2   The big banks' exposure to the big debtors: U S and U K banks' outstandings in Mexico, Brazil, Argentina and Venezuela as a proportion of capital at the end of 1984 (%)

BRITISH BANKS	
National Westminster	73
Barclays	62
Lloyds	165
Midland	205
AMERICAN BANKS	
Citicorp	140
BankAmerica	122
Chase Manhattan	142
Manufacturers Hanover	173
J. P. Morgan	103
Chemical	134
Bankers Trust	114
First Chicago	103

Sources: Figures for British banks are taken from City of London estimates. Those for American banks are drawn from Salomon Bros., Inc., *A Review of Bank Performance*, New York, 1985, Figures 30 and 51.

available to meet the contingency. The foreign currency deposits – overwhelmingly in dollars – of the British banks, for example, exceed the foreign currency reserves of the Bank of England by a factor of 35.[7] They are all ultimately dependent on the only source of dollar liquidity large enough to match the needs which would arise: the Federal Reserve System of the United States. The Federal Reserve, however, has limited powers to come to the rescue of banks out of its jurisdiction. No inter-governmental loan has ever been made on the scale which would be required in a crisis.

Banks throughout the Western world would be affected by a renewal of the debt crisis in Latin America for two reasons: both because they have lent directly to some of the largest borrowers and because they have also lent to the lead banks in London and New York which have been most active in the lending and whose own obligations would be at risk. The implication of American official figures, read together with the total figure for bank lending to individual countries assembled by the B I S in Basle, is that American banks account for about one-third of lending to Argentina, Brazil and Mexico. Some two-thirds is probably accounted for by loans from Europe and Japan. The German Bundesbank reported in May 1985, for example, that the West German banks were responsible for about 8.7 per cent of the outstanding private credit to twenty-five major debtor states, including 6.4 per cent of the claims on Brazil, 4.8 per cent of those on Mexico and 9.3·per cent of those on Argentina.[8] West Germany's overall exposure is thus very much in line with its share of the industrial world's economy, as appears to be the case with other countries.

The international position is inevitably complicated by lending through offshore centres such as the Cayman Islands and subsidiaries, but no one should be blind to the global nature of the heavy exposures of major Western banks to a handful of highly indebted developing countries. Moreover, the B I S figures show that the total cross-border claims of reporting banks *on one another* at the end of 1984 amounted to $1,268 billion.[9] The developed world's financial structures are inextricably linked, so that the malaise of one part cannot fail to be felt by others. In short, the whole world banking system is involved. No sizeable bank in any major country could escape the backlash.

The financial markets are increasingly troubled by the fragility of the banking system, not only because of the threat of Third World debt default but also because of the growing recognition that other lending at home and abroad is precarious. Figure 2 shows that the 1982 recession and its aftermath took an increasing toll of US banks. Bad debts within the United States provided the spark for the collapse of the Continental Illinois, which is still being nursed with a large capital injection from public funds. But it was Continental's lending to Latin America that prevented any other bank from taking it over. In 1982 Moody's bond survey downgraded the bonds of almost all the major money-centre banks, so that for the first time in recent memory the largest financial institutions in the most important market economy actually lost their triple-A credit status and access to funds at the most favoured rates which went with it. Moody's, the credit rating agency and the leading objective observer, clearly does not believe that the bank crisis is resolved.

Figure 2   The mounting casualties in U S banking

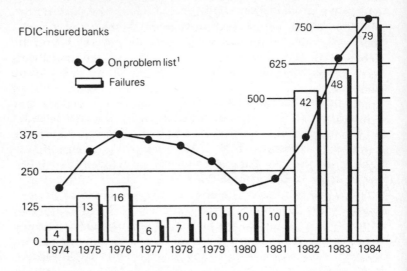

Note: [1] Number indicated by horizontal lines.

Sources: Business Week; Federal Deposit Insurance Corporation (F D I C).

Another indication of fragility is the gap between the interest rates paid by the Federal government on three-month Treasury bills and the rates paid by the banks on equivalent paper. After the Continental Illinois collapse this gap widened sharply for banks in all countries, even if they were uninvolved in the immediate crisis. Its subsequent narrowing merely reflects depositors' confidence that the Federal Reserve will not allow one of the lynchpin banks to fail. But the same confidence does not extend to the stock market, where the standing of all bank shares has deteriorated sharply compared with the rest of the market over the last decade, and the standing of the money-centre banks worsened disproportionately.

Nor, in reality, can it truthfully be said that the banks themselves are confident that the loans to the major debtors are safe. Whatever they may say publicly, the real guide to what they think is what they do. Since 1982 every major bank with exposure to the biggest debtors has tried to reduce it. The only reason why lending to the major debtors has gone up rather than down is because the IMF has organized an effective cartel which has insisted that the banks both 'reschedule', or renew, old debt *and* that they lend more money – that they increase their exposure in order to offset some of the interest due on the debt – or the Fund will not provide the country concerned with its money and supervision. Without the IMF, the debts to the banks would have suffered an immediate and dangerous loss of credibility. Thus the Mexican rescue package forced a 7 per cent increase in bank lending by all the banks who participated – so-called 'involuntary lending'. The IMF shows that of the $30 billion of new money extended by private institutions in 1983–4, only $7 billion was outside the framework of agreements to restructure debt.[10]

Yet if the banks *really* thought that the debtors were facing a problem merely of temporary illiquidity – a temporary lack of cash – rather than the more fundamental condition of insolvency or unwillingness to pay, then they would be quite prepared to lend the extra money instead of having their arms twisted. Behind the rhetoric of sound finance still lurks the fear of large losses. A vote of no confidence in the debtors by the banks, and by the other investors who are unwilling to lend them money voluntarily, implies an equal vote of no confidence in the banks themselves. After all, their solvency depends on the soundness of the debts they clearly find dubious.

The delicately poised pyramid of debt has proved sustainable since the Mexican crisis of 1982 only through the most extraordinary sacrifices by debtors and considerable and praiseworthy efforts by creditors and official institutions alike. However, some of the particular factors which have operated to ensure a 'co-operative' handling of the debt crisis may now be difficult to sustain.

If they are not sustained, the position of the Western financial system will be every bit as precarious as it was in the autumn of 1982. Indeed, it may only now be entering the period of most acute danger. These restraining factors affect both creditors and debtors, so we shall look at both in turn.

Let us take the banks first. Keeping the banks in line is an increasingly arduous task, first and foremost because of the enormous efforts involved in co-ordinating large groups of disparate interests and nationalities. The structure of the market is such that the banks themselves cannot be guaranteed to operate in their collective self-interest. As we have seen, it has been necessary for the IMF to insist that they collectively increase their exposure, thereby patching up the credibility of their old debt, rather than attempt individually to reduce it, thereby triggering a default.

One potent source of strain, however, is the small banks' incentive to extract an immediate repayment of their debt rather than merely extend some new lending in order to receive a slightly greater total of interest back from the debtor. Because small banks can claim that they could bear the loss of their lending, they can also plausibly insist that they will call the debtor into default unless they are repaid in full. They know, of course, that the big banks, with much more at stake, cannot possibly afford to declare a default and would prefer to extend even more new money themselves to release small banks from their exposure.

So far, the small banks have gone along with the IMF cartel, in part because of the opprobrium which might well be heaped upon them in banking circles if they did not, and in part because of more or less explicit threats from their central bankers. But several factors could change this. In the first place, the IMF's programmes are meant in theory to last only three years: it is not clear that the Fund will continue to organize the lenders' cartel when many of the agreements expire in 1986. Secondly, some groups of banks – for example, the Swiss – have made much greater efforts than, say, the Americans to build up their capital and may be increasingly tempted to pull out altogether.[11] In this respect, small countries may be rather similar to the small banks; they may be only too prepared to say that the debt is not their problem. Thirdly, the result of the rescheduling agreements of 1982 and 1983 is that a large hump of principal repayments will come due in 1987 and 1988, providing the small banks with ample excuse to attempt to pull out.[12]

If any such move takes place on a significant scale, the big banks will have to expose themselves even more to maintain the pretence that their old debt is being serviced, at the risk of depleted credibility and the loss of confidence of their depositors. In theory, the small banks would be threatening the debtors. In reality, their threat to call a default is directed at the banks and central banks simply because these are the only parties that can come up with the cash quickly enough to satisfy the small banks' demand for repayment.

Nor does the situation look more easily sustainable from the point of view of the debtors. Many observers – not least some of the officials in the Western institutions – have been surprised at the willingness of the debtor countries to make the substantial social and political sacrifices they have already made in order to cut imports and generate debt-service dollars. The IMF's adjustment programmes in 1982 and 1983 resulted first and foremost in a cut in imports through a cut in demand in the debtor countries – which inevitably also had the effect of cutting their output. Many of them were initially forced into sharper recession and drops in living standards than they endured even during the depression of 1929–31.

For Latin America as a whole, the cumulative drop in real Gross Domestic Product (GDP) per head of population between 1981 and 1984 was 8.9 per cent, an average which disguises drops of more than 10 per cent in Brazil between 1980 and 1983, in Mexico between 1981 and 1984 and in Chile, Bolivia and Uruguay in just one year, 1982.[13] These cuts in living standards were twice as great as those suffered by any industrial country over the same period and from levels of income which were one-third of the developed world's.

The debtors' recessions did, however, have the desired effect from the point of view of the Fund and the creditors; they released large amounts of foreign exchange for the service of debt. Table 3 shows the resource flow – mainly new lending minus interest payments – to and from the debtor countries over the period from 1977 to 1984, with IMF projections for 1985 and 1986.[14]

As the table shows, the seven major borrowers and the western-hemisphere countries of Central and South America all enjoyed a resource flow from the advanced world to them until 1982. There should be no surprise that this was the case: flows

Table 3 *The resource flow to and from the debtor countries 1977–84 and IMF projections 1985–6*
($ billion)

	1977	1978	1979	1980	1981	1982	1983	1984	1985	1986
INDEBTED DEVELOPING COUNTRIES										
Current account deficit	36.9	56.8	61.7	77.0	112.6	102.9	59.4	37.9	38.2	36.7
Net investment income including interest	−11.3	−14.7	−21.1	−30.3	−44.2	−56.5	−56.9	−60.4	−61.4	−60.0
Resource flow	25.6	42.1	40.6	46.7	68.4	46.4	2.5	−22.5	−23.2	−23.3
Resource flow as percentage of exports of goods and services	9.8%	14%	10.3%	9.1%	12.8%	9.2%	0.5%	−4.1%	−4%	−3.7%
MAJOR BORROWERS (7 countries)[1]										
Current account deficit	9.5	18.4	22.3	26.5	35.7	39.8	10.9	1.5	4.0	3.0
Net investment income including interest	−6.2	−8.3	−12.1	−18.0	−26.1	−34.2	−33.4	−36.0	−35.7	−33.4
Resource flow	3.3	10.1	10.2	8.5	9.6	5.6	−22.5	−34.5	−31.7	−30.4
Resource flow as percentage of exports of goods and services	4.8%	12.9%	10.1%	6.3%	6.2%	4%	−16.3%	−22.7%	−19.5%	−17.3%
WESTERN HEMISPHERE (33 countries)										
Current account deficit	11.6	19.4	21.7	29.3	43.1	42.1	11.7	5.5	7.5	6.8
Net investment income including interest	−5.4	−7.5	−10.8	−15.5	−24.2	−33.6	−32.5	−34.3	−33.7	−31.5
Resource flow	6.2	11.9	10.9	13.8	18.9	8.5	−20.8	−28.8	−26.2	−24.7
Resource flow as percentage of exports of goods and services	9.6%	16.6%	11.4%	11.1%	14%	7.1%	−18.1%	−23%	−19.8%	−17.5%

Note: [1] Argentina, Indonesia, Mexico, Venezuela, Brazil, South Korea, Philippines.

of capital to developing countries have been a feature of economic progress since time immemorial. Without such flows, the economic development of the United States, Canada and Australia – to name but three cases – would have been seriously impeded. The surprise is that the resource flow turned sharply negative in 1983, leading to a negative transfer from the developing countries to their advanced-country creditors. In the case of the seven biggest borrowers, this perverse transfer amounts to between 16.3 per cent and 22.6 per cent of their exports of goods and services in each year from 1983 to 1986. For the western-hemisphere countries, it varies from 17.5 per cent to 23 per cent. The sums of money involved – nearly $35 billion for the big seven in 1984 alone – are enormous by any measure, representing cash which could have been used instead to increase imports, demand, output and living standards.

The optimists argue that the very fact that these countries have been prepared to accept such pain in order to 'restore their international creditworthiness' (to make negative transfers) is testament enough to their continued willingness to do so. That is a dangerously complacent view on several counts. It is clear, for example, that a more or less permanent default on obligations to the Western banks has never been the immediate most favoured option of any debtor: it would inevitably be a leap into unplumbed darkness. The decision to service their debts has, however, been made in the hope of other consequences.

The first hope of the debtors is for some form of official relief on their debt by the Western authorities. They also hope for official contributions or guarantees to increase the amount of lending and reduce the extent to which trade surpluses have to meet the need for debt-service dollars. Their third objective could well be substantially softer IMF terms, with more Fund credit being made available over longer periods. Default or repudiation of their debts may be the fourth option – ranking ahead of acceptance of the present tough approach by the Western institutions – but the debtors would still attempt to give themselves negotiating time to explore the three options they favour instead. The IMF's travails with Argentina, or repeated reneging on letters of intent to the IMF by Brazil, are obvious instances of the process.

There is another element of fragility in the debtors' position. The hopes of the optimists have rested squarely on the idea that the initial period of pain, in which the debtors' contribution to debt service was overwhelmingly generated by cuts in Latin America's merchandise imports (in volume terms) of 19 per cent in 1982 and 27 per cent in 1983,[15] would be rapidly succeeded by a period when extra foreign exchange would instead come through increased export volume. Indeed, the export volume of Latin America did rise by 8.6 per cent in 1983 and by a further 9.8 per cent in 1984, bringing jobs in its wake to offset some of the losses of the slump.

However, those increases in exports were extraordinarily dependent on the buoyancy of just one major market: the United States. Between 1982 and 1984 Latin America's exports rose by $11 billion, with 87 per cent of the increase going to the fast-expanding United States market.[16] (By contrast, in 1980–82 Latin America sent only 32.5 per cent of all its exports to the United States.)[17] This immense reliance on the American market could only too easily backfire as United States growth slows down or if it corrects a trade deficit which almost every analyst, including the IMF, believes to be unsustainable in the medium term. As the Bonn Western Economic Summit in 1985 made clear, the European countries (which accounted for 19.5 per cent of Latin America's exports in 1980–82) have no intention of taking measures which are likely to stimulate their growth in the short term. There is little hope of other developed countries taking up the slack if America slows down.

Perhaps the most compelling reason why the debtors have so far accepted the austerity and the negative transfers demanded of them is the immense damage which a sudden contraction of trade credit could do to their economies. This point was well summed up by Mario-Henrique Simonsen, the Brazilian economist and former minister, when he pointed out that a tough strategy of default by a debtor would lead creditors to react by

cutting commercial credit facilities, and forcing the country to pay for most of its imports on a cash basis. Since there is a [time] lag in export receipts behind shipments, the country would have imposed on it a resource surplus worth, perhaps, four or six months' imports. This is a much more stringent effort than what is required by an IMF adjustment programme. When the country is illiquid, it leads to a highly painful and inefficient balance of payments adjustment through import rationing.[18]

In other words, until now the debtors' main private creditors have had the powerful weapon of refusing to finance trade. This 'short leash' has meant that at any point over the last few years the option of *not* going along with IMF programmes, even when they have meant running substantial trade surpluses and perverse transfers, has been worse than the option of sticking with them. Instead of a slow transition to large and regular resource transfers to the rich creditor countries, the debtors would have been forced immediately to endure even greater hardships.

That factor, however, is slowly changing. Over a number of years the debtor countries are able to insure themselves against any such short, sharp shock in at least four ways. They can build up their reserves of foreign currencies, allowing them to finance out of their own resources the time lag between import payments and export receipts; they can gradually skew more of their trade away from a cash basis, often in dollars, and towards crude exchanges, or barter trade; they can accumulate stocks of key imports; and they can embark on programmes of import substitution, whereby they attempt to produce goods which would otherwise have to be imported. (A good example of long standing is Brazil's attempts to fuel cars and trucks by gasohol – fuel made from sugar – rather than crude oil.) Import substitution tends to be a longer-term undertaking, while the accumulation of import stocks is difficult to disaggregate from published figures of the usual inventory upturn which took place in many of the debtor economies in 1984. But there is evidence that both reserves and counter-trade are mounting.

The IMF's figures show that the main debtors have been building up their foreign exchange reserves very quickly. In 1984 the total foreign exchange reserves of the developing countries rose by $22 billion, the largest increase on record.[19] The seven largest debtors built up their reserves by $16 billion between 1982 and 1984, taking foreign-exchange reserves as a proportion of annual imports from a low point of 12.5 per cent, or one and a half months of import purchases, to 24.9 per cent, or three months. The build-up in the western hemisphere has been as dramatic, with reserve cover for imports rising from 17.3 per cent in 1982 to 31 per cent in 1984 – nearly four months' worth of import purchases.

Trade which does not rely on money is also rising. So-called counter-trade includes straight barter agreements to swop, say,

coffee for machine tools, and more complicated buy-back production agreements under which machinery is exported in exchange for part of the resulting products. The evidence for such
practices is by definition hard to collect, but the United Nations
Conference on Trade and Development (UNCTAD) estimates
range from 15 per cent to 30 per cent of world trade, with a
central estimate that 'counter-trade's share in world trade probably significantly exceeds 15 per cent. Moreover, it is widely
thought that the share of developing countries in such trade is
increasing.'[20] A typical example is a counter-trade deal between
Nigeria and Brazil, concluded in September 1984, to swap Niger-
ian crude oil for Brazilian vehicle-assembly kits from Volkswagen
do Brasil as well as food, spares and industrial raw materials.
Originally valued at $500 million, negotiations were under way
at the time of writing to increase the deal to about $950 million.[21]

The conditions under which a moratorium on debt can be
seriously contemplated by some of the major debtors are therefore only now beginning to be met. That is not to argue that
defaults or moratoria are going to become unequivocally attractive options: many factors need to be carefully weighed, not
least the likelihood of a change in Western official attitudes.
(The question of default is more fully explored in Chapter 7.)
But it is undeniable that domestic pressures in the large debtor
countries are far from subsiding. Unemployment is in many
cases continuing to rise from the very high levels of the slump.
Population growth continues to outstrip the growth of debtors'
economies. Living standards, as measured by real GDP per
head, fell in a dozen Latin American countries in 1984 and were
unchanged for the continent as a whole.

In the Latin American political systems, just as in those of the
more developed countries, there also tends to be a time-lag
between economic reality and the political debate. Until 1984 the
question of debt and growth had been treated largely as a technical
one best left to, and understood by, finance ministry officials and
the central bankers. That is no longer the case. Debt is becoming
a central political issue in many of the Latin American countries,
and it can only be expected that the negative transfers which are
at the centre of the West's view of how the debt crisis should be
resolved will come under increasingly critical gaze. Neither the
economics nor the politics of debt justifies peace of mind.

3

THE ORIGINS OF THE CRISIS I:
THE DEMAND FOR CREDIT

History is a good teacher but there are inattentive pupils.

GEORGE J. STIGLER

Debt does not get paid; debt gets rolled.

DELFIM NETO

For nearly ten years Third World debt was rolled over. As soon as one lot of loans matured, there was a bevy of willing bankers ready to extend new loans to repay it. The rolling loans which gathered no loss made everyone happy. So long as everyone believed that the process could go on, it went on. Not for nothing is the root of the word 'credit' the Latin verb *credere*, meaning 'to believe'.

In 1982 the snowball of lending which had taken Third World debt from about $130 billion in 1973 to some $612 billion nine years later came to a halt. In August 1982 the Mexican government announced an immediate moratorium on its foreign-currency debt: it had been unable to raise new loans big enough to repay the debts which were becoming due. Within months the markets which had lavished funds on the debtor countries were closed to them. Some four countries a year had needed to postpone repayments of due debt principal between 1975 and 1980, an early warning which the advanced countries failed to heed. By 1983 the number had reached twenty-one. The debt could no longer be rolled, and the recriminations began. In 1985 Brazil instituted state criminal proceedings against ex-planning minister Mr Delfim Neto, who was accused of negligence and the mishandling of public money.

The next two chapters are about how and why the snowball rolled for so long. These are questions of more than historical interest, for the causes of the debt crisis provide a rich seam for the present-day debate over prospects and cures. There is nothing in logic, of course, which would suggest that those who are responsible for the crisis are necessarily capable of resolving it. Nor are they the most obvious source of sound advice. Governments, banks and commentators had a sorry record in the years preceding the crisis. But, inevitably, policy prescriptions tend to flow from different analyses of causes.

For some, the evidence of the 1970s and early 1980s indicates that the debtors brought the crisis upon themselves through bad policy and wasteful spending. By implication, much of the cure lies in their own efforts to redress their predicament. For others, the build-up of debt was a consequence of the repeated external shocks administered to the debtors by two sets of oil price rises and the depressive financial policies which the industrial countries subsequently pursued to damp down the inflationary effects. In this case, the creditors must share the burden of the aftermath. The stress is on getting the world environment right so that industrial and developing countries alike can prosper. A third strand of analysis pinpoints the commercial nature of the debt itself and the inherent instability of world capital markets, which are prone to cycles of feast and famine in the treatment of borrowers. This view in turn implies that a part of the solution must lie in regulating the flows of funds to the developing countries so that they match their needs in a regular and reliable manner.

These three themes, however, are not mutually exclusive. Indeed, any analysis which failed to highlight the external shocks such as the oil price rises in explaining the rapid increase in the developing countries' demand for loans would be seriously misleading. Equally, it is clear that one part of the demand for loans went side by side with domestic policies which were, at least in retrospect, mistaken, particularly in the case of some of the Latin American problem debtors and in the later part of the build-up of debt before the crisis of 1982. But demand is only one part of the equation: whatever borrowing the developing world might have wanted to do would have been to no avail without a Western financial system which accommodated it. To attempt to 'blame' either over-borrowing by the debtors or over-lending by the creditors is to ignore the fact that you cannot have one without the other: it takes two sides to sign a loan agreement. If the debtors made errors, responsibility must also be borne by the lending banks and the government officials who encouraged them. In this chapter we look at the 'demand factors' for debt. In the next chapter we examine the supply side which also made the lending possible.

The obvious starting-point for an analysis of the debtors' demand for funds is an examination of what they spent the money on, but innumerable analyses, reaching fundamentally different conclusions, suggest that this is far from the simple question it looks. For example, the secretariat of the General Agreement on Tariffs and Trade (GATT) has maintained that the build-up of debt did not have a counterpart of real investment: a significant proportion was 'dead-weight debt', with the implication that it was hard to see how it could be serviced. The IMF and some independent researchers have responded by seeking to prove statistically a close correspondence between flows of commercial credits and private investment in the developing countries. Yet another study has come to the conclusion that the build-up of debt was exactly paralleled by the build-up in Third World armaments spending.[1]

That these often sophisticated mathematical exercises can come to such opposite conclusions is testament to one factor alone: all money is fungible, but foreign exchange is particularly fungible: the object of the lending may have been one thing, but something else entirely is delivered in its place. A bank, for example, may have thought its money was going on a steelworks, but the reality may have been that the steel boss and his daughters instead spent a long holiday in Bermuda and bought a villa in Miami.

Take a recent case from Britain: a few years ago the Bank of England was mystified by the very large increase in mortgages on houses which appeared to lead neither to new houses nor to a sharp rise in house prices, despite the fact that it is a golden rule of the building society movement that it lends money *only* to buy or improve houses. The solution to the mystery appears to be that people borrowed more money to buy cars, holidays and hi-fi systems. In some cases they did so merely by asking for a bigger mortgage on the grounds of some specious home improvement. In other cases they requested a bigger mortgage than they needed when they moved house in order to release some of the capital from their previous home for other uses.

It is even more difficult to tie down the end use of foreign exchange. First of all, there is the difficulty which applies to any domestic example. Let us say that an American bank is keen to finance a new hotel complex in a developing country at a cost of 2 billion pesos. The deal is signed, and construction work begins. But is the hotel company really using all the money to build the hotel, or would it have built it anyway and paid its chambermaids less? With foreign exchange there is an additional problem: you do not even know who has used the money, let alone whether it was used efficiently. Let us say the hotel company's loan is for $1 million. As it happens, the company needs to import only bath taps and various other fixtures from abroad, so that the new complex uses up a mere 1 per cent of the $1 million. All the rest is converted into pesos to pay for materials and construction workers. Nobody knows what happens to the rest of the dollars: they simply go into the country's kitty of foreign exchange for the purchase of imports, foreign holidays or New York safe deposits.

In this sense, most foreign-currency lending, which is rarely tied to specific imports, is merely general lending to the residents of the country concerned, in the hope that they will conduct themselves in such a manner as to meet their obligations. It is, in other words, finance to meet a deficit on the current account of the balance of payments, a capital outflow on the capital account or an accumulation of official reserves. If it is used to sustain a higher level of demand and imports than would otherwise have been the case, it is certainly true that foreign currency lending will be a boon to growth. It will thus almost certainly encourage investment, which is undertaken in the expectation of profitable demand for the resulting products. But there is no necessary and direct link between foreign-currency lending and investment, let alone the type of investment necessary to earn the foreign exchange to service the loan.

Essentially, the pace of growth is dependent largely on the sustainable growth of its imports. If domestic demand in an economy increases rapidly – an essential condition, in most cases, for an increase in domestic output and employment – then that demand tends in part to go into imports from abroad and to require foreign exchange. This is not merely a function of increases in consumer goods. Imports are also crucial to the supply capacity of economies, allowing them to increase production. In Latin America, for example, more than half of all imports consist of intermediate goods and raw materials which are used in the production process. At the same time, capital goods – machine tools, fork-lift trucks and so forth – account for about a quarter of Latin American imports.[2]

One way of assuring high import growth is through high export growth by means of devaluation, a slower growth of domestic than international costs, industrial policy and other measures. But the pace of such adjustment is slow and uncertain and is rarely fast enough to accord with development ambitions or potential. The build-up of debt during the 1970s reflected in part a decision by the debtors to afford more imports and to maintain a higher rate of growth than would otherwise have been possible. There was even a phrase for it: 'debt-led growth'.

Because foreign-currency lending is balance-of-payments finance, any analysis which claims that the build-up of such-and-such a country's debt has been related solely to armaments or investment or anything else is implicitly claiming that it knows exactly what the path of the economy would have been if the lending had not taken place. With modern statistical techniques it may eventually be possible to develop such analyses and attribute effects to particular causes. But the development of econometric models of the Third World is not yet advanced enough, nor uncontroversial enough, to make bold claims. Nor is it easy to capture political decisions about public spending in such models, and much of the lending and spending in the Third World has been very political. It is not therefore fruitful to attempt to provide a dollar-by-dollar account of where the debt went to, though we can sketch out some of the factors in the demand for foreign currency by the debtors, with some tentative guesses at orders of magnitude.

The first and obvious candidate is the deterioration in the world economic environment. Oil prices had fallen from $1.50 a barrel in 1960 to $1.30 a barrel in 1970, a substantial real decline after allowing for general inflation.[3] From 1971 the oil price began to edge upwards. The collapse of the Bretton Woods system of fixed exchange rates was widely heralded as allowing governments to break free of the 'constraint' of holding to a fixed parity, which in effect meant ensuring that domestic demand did not grow so rapidly as to suck in excessive imports, open up a trade deficit and weaken the currency by unloading it on foreigners. The relaxation of that constraint, together with the unfortunate bunching in late 1972 and early 1973 of the largest number of elections in the developed world since the war, set the conditions for a substantial expansion of demand in the industrial world.[4]

Commodity prices inevitably began to rise, since the supply of agricultural products and many other raw materials is, in the short term, unresponsive to price rises. In 1972 commodity prices rose by 13 per cent and by a further 53 per cent in 1973.[5] Oil prices edged up to $2.70; the Yom Kippur war in late 1973 provided the occasion for the beginnings of an effective OPEC cartel. The further rise in oil prices to $10 and above in 1974 and 1975 had immediate effects on trade accounts around the world. The oil-exporting countries moved from a surplus on their current account of $7 billion in 1973 to one of $68 billion in 1974. This inevitably had its mirror-image in the deterioration of the current accounts of the oil importers. The industrial countries saw a current-account surplus of $12 billion in 1973 deteriorate to a deficit of $24 billion in 1974. By 1975 they had managed to claw back their position to a surplus of $6 billion, due in part to an enormous expansion of exports to the oil exporters and in part to a contraction of domestic demand which in turn reduced imports.

The impact of the oil price rise on developing countries which did not export oil was even greater. Crude oil tended to be a larger share of their total import bill than that of the industrial countries: their deficit on the current account rose from $11 billion in 1973 to $37 billion in 1974. They had to start borrowing to pay higher oil prices. But they were then hit in 1975 by the slow-down in industrial country demand, which cut 19 per cent off commodity prices, slowed their growth and helped increase their current-account deficit to $46 billion. If they had cut this deficit by engineering sharp cuts in domestic demand, as the advanced countries did, they would have suffered large losses of output and applied a brake to their development. The current-account deficits of the non-oil developing countries were gradually reduced by export growth in 1976 and 1977, but in 1979 they were hit once again by oil price rises which took Saudi crude from $13 a barrel in 1978 to $32.50 in 1981. For the non-oil developing countries, oil as a percentage of spending on imports went from 5.9 per cent in 1973 to 21 per cent in 1981. Despite the small change in oil import volume, the rise in oil prices was enough to turn oil into one of the largest and fastest-growing items of imports.

The importance of the oil factor in stimulating the demand for foreign-currency loans can be seen from calculations by Professor William Cline, which show that the extra cost of oil imports above 1973 levels cost the non-oil developing countries a cumulative $260 billion up to 1982.[6] That figure does not make any allowance for the interest charges on each year's additional oil bill, which would take the total to some $335 billion out of an increase in debt on IMF estimates of $482 billion. This was one side of the process of 'recycling': OPEC earned foreign currency on its exports of oil faster than it could spend it, so it saved the cash, placing it in large part on deposit with Western banks. They in turn lent it on to the oil-importing Third World to finance imports of higher-priced oil. (This unregulated lending effectively underwrote each increased exaction by the oil cartel. It also artificially weakened the dollar against other currencies, as the lending was overwhelmingly denominated in the American currency.)

Oil, though, does not explain everything on the demand side. After all, two of the largest debtors, Mexico and Venezuela, were net oil exporters during the debt build-up, in part to finance the increased imports of capital equipment for the oil industry. In the latter part of the decade another important external factor was the rise in interest rates. For the major middle-income debtors this raised the cost of 'new money' – any new loan extended by a bank, even if primarily to repay a maturing old loan or interest; it also raised the cost of the overwhelming bulk of their debt, which had been contracted at variable interest rates depending on the interest the banks had to pay for wholesale deposits in London – the London Interbank Offered Rate (LIBOR) – generally for three- or six-month deposits. Throughout most of the 1970s relatively relaxed monetary policies in the industrial countries kept real interest rates (i.e. interest rates after allowing for inflation) low or even negative: that is to say, the interest payments which the debtors had to hand over on a given amount of debt failed to compensate the lenders for the erosion in the worth of the principal caused by price rises.

After touching a low point in 1976, however, United States inflation began to edge upwards and with it went interest rates, though still, for many borrowers, remaining negative in real terms. The first effect was one of cash flow. In order to keep the inflation-adjusted level of debt constant, let alone secure the same positive net transfer,* a debtor had to borrow more 'new money' than before to offset higher interest rates. A process began of giving with one hand and taking back with the other.

The second and more important shock was a rise in *real* interest rates from 1979 onwards as the industrial world attempted to offset the effects of the second oil shock on inflation. The result was that the debtors' net outflows of profits, dividends and interest payments rose from $15 billion in 1978 to $44 billion in 1981.[7] On UNCTAD calculations, the rise in interest rates between 1976–9 and 1980–82 added $41 billion to the total stock of Third World debt at the end of the period.[8] When it is now argued that higher interest rates alone upset the applecart, the implication is that the system was sustainable only with interest rates which slowly allowed the debt to evaporate. The reality, however, was that the rise in interest rates was responsible for a small part of the debt build-up and made its impact on a system which was fundamentally unsound for other reasons.

A further oil price rise and the rise in real interest rates were only part of the shock delivered to the debtors between 1978 and 1982. Once again, the effect of Western policy aimed at countering renewed inflation by depressing demand was to cause a sharp drop in the value of Third World exports. Even the upper-middle-income countries of Latin America remain strongly dependent on commodity exports. In Brazil soya beans, coffee and iron ore accounted for 83 per cent of merchandise exports in 1981–2.[9] In Argentina wheat, corn and beef provide one-third of exports. In Chile copper alone accounts for nearly half. As the industrial world went into recession, commodity prices fell by one-quarter between 1980 and 1982.[10] Rising oil prices, higher nominal and real interest rates, sluggish developed-country markets, a rise in the dollar in which most

---

* These terms require clarification. A net transfer is synonymous with 'new money' minus interest payments and principal repayments, or 'new money' minus debt service. Net 'new money' (net new borrowing) is 'new money' minus repayments of maturing loans but *not* minus interest payments – the same as the change in total debt outstanding over a period. Debt service comprises interest and principal repayments on loans, even if partially or fully offset by new loans.

of the debt was denominated and falling export prices added up to a formidable shock, diminishing the sources of foreign exchange while increasing demand for it.

It is clear, however, that the attempt to compensate for external shocks to debtor economies was not the only use for foreign-currency finance and that some of the other explanations are decidedly less flattering to the Third World's policymakers. Two classes of policy decision added unnecessarily to outstanding debt by the time of the 1982 crisis. (Alternatively, they can be seen as having reduced potential economic growth for the given increase in debt.) The first was the clear instances of political decisions to increase arms imports, which could not produce domestic investment, still less provide capacity which would increase the foreign-exchange earning power needed to service debt. The second were macro-economic policy errors which encouraged imports, discouraged exports and stimulated the build-up of private capital abroad by Third World residents.

Arms imports by the Third World more than trebled in real dollar terms between 1962–71 and 1972–81, totalling in the latter decade some $74 billion in 1975 prices.[11] This enormous increase was due in part to the insatiable hunger of many Third World regimes, particularly military ones, for the latest armaments technology. But the arms suppliers were also keen to sell material. For example, the economies of scale reaped by Dassault through selling 350 Mirage IIIs abroad are estimated to have reduced the unit cost of the 200 aircraft bought by the French airforce by 25 per cent.[12] Foreign military sales provided budget, employment and balance-of-payments gains to the vendor countries.

Whether extra arms imports contributed to the build-up of debt is dubious, however. The crude comparison looks like this: the extra arms imports in 1972–81, compared with the previous ten years, amounted to some $51.1 billion in 1975 dollars,[13] while the debt of the Third World expanded on the same basis by around $200 billion. One study has argued that around one-quarter of the debt accumulated is due to weapons imports.[14] Another study by the Rand Corporation, which looks specifically at the soft loans offered by Western governments for arms imports, concludes that around 8 per cent of the oustanding Third World debt at the end of 1979 was due to arms purchases.[15]

However, one problem with this type of aggregate estimate for the Third World as a whole is that it does not attempt to match the areas where the debt built up with the areas which absorbed most arms. The Middle East took 46 per cent of Third World arms sales in 1972 to 1981, yet most of the purchasers were OPEC countries with large net overseas asset (rather than debtor) positions. It is much harder to ascribe a large role to arms sales in the plight of the main problem debtors in Latin America. Arms sales to this region *did* rise more quickly than sales to the Third World as a whole, but they had started from a very low relative base. Comparing 1962–71 with 1972–81, the actual increase in Latin American arms imports was some $6 billion in 1975 prices, which does not go a long way to explain an increase of around $115 billion in Latin American debt (in 1975 prices). In addition, there are the fungibility problems we have mentioned: would the arms have been bought anyway? Furthermore, there were actually foreign-exchange offsets through arms exports on the part of some of the biggest debtors – notably South Korea and Brazil.

The indictment of bad macro-economic policy is much clearer. Many of the debtors embarked on the chronic governmental search for a soft option. Bad policy certainly did worsen the trade-off between growth and debt, though much more so in, say, Argentina and Mexico than in Brazil. There is obviously room for argument about what constitutes a legitimate attempt to offset the impact of external shocks like oil price rises or weaker industrial country growth and what constitutes wilful folly in the face of economic realities.

Few analysts would doubt, though, that Mexico's attempt to maintain an 8.2 per cent average annual growth between 1978 and 1981, when the industrial world and oil markets were clearly heading for a period of weakness, falls into the latter category. Mexican confidence in future growth was high and was spurred on by successive announcements of rising oil reserves. It became extremely difficult for the finance ministry to hold off requests for increased spending. With a presidential election not far off, the budget deficit of spending over revenue rose from 6.9 per cent of Gross National Product (GNP) in 1980 to 16.3 per cent in 1982.[16] The equivalent US figure which caused such a furore in 1984 was 3.2 per cent. The Mexican government also allowed the peso to become seriously over-valued. Despite rises in costs and prices that were far more frequent than those of their main trading partners, the Mexicans failed to devalue their currency in line, contributing to the deterioration in non-oil exports and to an import boom.

In Argentina and in Chile the governments tried for a while to stop their currencies from devaluing in line with the difference between their inflation rates and those abroad, in order to moderate import price rises and to stem inflation. But this experiment with the 'law of one price' – the theory that foreign competition would rapidly and fairly costlessly force domestic producers to slow down their price rises – had the predictable effect of increasing the amounts of imports required to fund given growth rates, while at the same time uncompetitive exports increased the need for debt dollars on the other side of the trade accounts. The losses of price competitiveness, or rise in the real exchange rate, were in some cases enormous: more than 60 per cent in Argentina and 41 per cent in Mexico between 1980 and 1983.[17] In the Chilean case the currency was arguably over-valued at the beginning of the 1980s and deserved its downward correction in 1981, but between 1981 and 1983 the government once again' allowed the peso to appreciate in real terms by one-third. The losses of competitiveness, when measured solely by comparison with the Americans rather than with a weighted basket of trading partners, were even more drastic. Although the dollar rose throughout this period, many of these countries were pegged to the US currency, and their inflation rates were far higher than the American rate and rising. Brazil was generally an exception to the catalogue of exchange-rate mismanagement by some of the major Latin American debtors save for a brief and ill-advised attempt to limit the devaluation of the cruzeiro in 1980, but even that country found its real exchange rate against the dollar up by 34 per cent between 1980 and 1983.

The over-valuations of many of the most important Latin American currencies, particularly against the dollar, did not simply make imports cheaper. Exports, when priced in foreign currency, became more expensive. Over-valuation also made overseas assets – the Miami apartment and American Treasury bill – relatively cheaper. To the extent, too, that the over-valuations looked unsustainable, the temptation to move assets out of the domestic currency and into dollars was overwhelming.

The flight of private capital was enormous: between 1979 and 1982 it is estimated at $27.9 billion from Mexico, $20.9 billion from Venezuela and $11.4 billion from Argentina.[18] This capital flight, which is reportedly still continuing, surreptitiously, by the false pricing of imports and exports, inevitably added directly to the need for foreign currency and debt, and in the most wasteful manner. Not only did a trade deficit and interest payments have to be financed but also private overseas asset-building. Effectively, Latin American governments were building up official foreign-currency debt in part to finance the private tax-free caches of their citizens abroad, with little or no let or hindrance from capital controls, restrictions on convertibility or even limits on private foreign-currency borrowing, the proceeds of which could be promptly sent abroad. No capital controls can be wholly effective, but sound policies and some controls would undoubtedly have mitigated the problem.

In this chapter we have looked at the origins of the debt crisis from the point of view of the debtor countries and their demand for foreign currency. The problem of fungibility – the difficulty of tracing exactly how foreign currency lending was used – makes any attempt at precise quantification specious. However, a number of factors in the demand for debt can be highlighted.

First and foremost were the shocks administered to the debtor countries by events in the world economy. The rise in oil prices meant that most developing countries had to pay considerably more for a given amount of oil imports. The reaction of the advanced countries to the inflationary effects of the oil price rises in turn depressed world commodity markets and cut the prices of a given quantity of most debtors' exports. The dividing line between sensible borrowing to ease the pace of adjustments to these new realities, so as to minimize disruption to output and living standards, and an obstinate refusal to adjust at all, or even to adjust in the wrong direction, is essentially a subjective one. Nevertheless, it seems clear that in the final years before the Mexican crisis in 1982 some of the Latin American debtors pursued policies which increased their need for foreign currency and that this too was a factor in the debt build-up. For every borrower, however, there is also a lender. In the next chapter we turn to the factors which encouraged the advanced countries' banks to supply funds to the developing countries during the 1970s.

4

THE ORIGINS OF THE CRISIS 2:
THE SUPPLY OF CREDIT

A 'sound' banker, alas! is not one who foresees danger,
and avoids it, but one who, when he is ruined,
is ruined in a conventional and orthodox way
along with his fellows, so that no one can really blame him.
It is necessarily part of the business
of a banker to maintain appearances, and to profess
a conventional respectability, which is more than human.
Life-long practices of this kind make them
the most romantic and the least realistic of men.

JOHN MAYNARD KEYNES

Tis better to have lent and lost
than never to have lent at all.

HENRY C. WALLICH (1943)

What were the mechanisms which made possible the supply of
bank lending on the scale necessary to build the Third World's
debt mountain? The first was the growth of the so-called Euro-
market in international deposit-taking and lending. The term is
now misleading, since the market effectively covers the globe
and extends to all the major currencies, though still predomi-
nantly in the dollar. A Euro-dollar is any dollar that is held in
banks outside the United States and thus outside the direct
control of the American monetary authorities.

The Euro-market had begun in a small way during the 1950s,
partly in reaction to the desire of communist countries to deposit
their surplus dollars outside the United States but also as a
result of the growing role of the dollar as the world's trading
and investment currency. It was boosted during the 1960s by
the penalties imposed on American-based lending. But its
growth really accelerated with the first oil shock and the deposits
of the OPEC countries which they preferred not, or were not
able, to spend. Deposits from abroad with banks reporting to
the BIS rose from a mere $55 billion in 1965 to $650 billion in
1975 and to more than $2100 billion at the end of 1984.[1]

Many of these deposits merely reflected business between the banks, but the net average annual growth rate of deposits other than those from reporting banks was still 25–30 per cent a year. As the deposits rolled in, the banks hastened to lend. Later the lending itself created new deposits which could serve as a base for new lending. This is to make no more than the well-known point that in any banking system every loan creates a new deposit in the system as a whole. As fast as the borrowers spend money, the recipients bank it. The original loan can be multiplied many times as the process of lending and depositing continues. One check to the almost infinite expansion of lending and deposit-taking is the legal requirement in most countries for banks to hold a certain minimum of their deposits in liquid assets like cash or easily tradeable government bills. There are also similar rules about the ratio of lending, or assets, to the bank's own capital. These have the effect of damping down each successive rise in loans and deposits.

But the advantage of the Euro-market, as perceived by the banks, was the very absence of such regulation. The restrictions of national systems were lacking. The extent of credit creation was to a large degree dependent on the banks' own definition of their capital and reserve requirements, which in turn depended on their confidence in their assets. The less risk they perceived, the more the money-go-round could accelerate unchecked. Moreover, the deposits of a particular currency held abroad by foreigners (and, one suspects, by residents of the country) often do not figure in the monetary aggregates which are meant to provide a guide to interest-rate policy.

Effectively, the West's monetary authorities turned a blind eye to the expansion of Euro-market credit during this period. This was due in part merely to official sluggishness in keeping up with a rapidly changing financial world. In addition, most of the Euro-market was situated in London, and the British authorities had little incentive to curb what appeared to be an important and growing source of the City's foreign-exchange earnings. Net international bank credit (excluding loans to other BIS-reporting banks) rose from $260 billion in 1975 to $1265 billion in 1984,[2] a rate far in excess of any measure of international inflation.

The business of lending to the Third World was, and is, highly profitable on paper. But the profits depend on maintaining the belief among bankers, their shareholders and depositors that there is no risk involved. Two technical developments in the Euro-market protracted the suspension of disbelief. Both of these made their appearance in 1969 and are attributed to a banker called Minos Zombanakis, who set up a merchant-bank offshoot in London of Rothschild's and Manufacturers Hanover of New York.[3] He was asked to raise an $80 million loan for Iran, a sum which was large at the time. He succeeded by sharing it with other banks, thus giving birth to the syndicated loan. The advantage to the banks was that they were able to take a piece of many different loans to different countries, thus appearing to spread their risk by not becoming excessively exposed to any one debtor.

The second innovation later the same year was to move from fixed interest-rate loans – with which the bank took the risk that interest rates might rise and the loan might become less profitable or even loss-making – to variable interest-rate loans, where the rate payable by the borrower was a fixed margin, or 'spread', over the cost of the funds to the banks. Whatever happened to the cost of funds, the banks were thus assured of turning a profit – provided, of course, that the borrowers could be guaranteed to continue to service their debt.

Any doubt on this score was waved aside by some of the most active proponents of international bank lending, notably the aggressive banker who was responsible for building up Citibank's international network during the 1960s and who became head of the corporation in 1967. Under Mr Walter Wriston's leadership during the 1970s Citibank set the pace and the standards by which the international activities of the other leading American banks were judged. It was Wriston above all who is associated with the theory which was later to be dignified by the title 'sovereign-risk hypothesis': 'Bankruptcy is a procedure,' Wriston said in Lausanne in 1981, 'developed in Western law to forgive the obligations of a person or a company that owes more than it has. Any country, however badly off, will "own" more than it "owes".' Countries simply could not go bankrupt; countries did not disappear; even if they occasionally had some short-term cash-flow difficulties, the cure would be 'sound programs and the time to let them work'. In the end the debt would always be repaid because the markets would regain confidence, and it could be redeemed if only by issuing more debt. After all, Wriston said, this was the reality behind every issue of a US government Treasury bill: no one expected the bill to be repaid on maturity other than by the issue of another. Wriston and Delfim Neto were as one in arguing that debt did not get paid, it got rolled.[4]

A number of flaws in this argument were to be exposed only too brutally a year later, at the time of the Mexican crisis, but history shows that whatever else happens to countries, it is far from impossible for them to stop servicing their debts and even to repudiate them. Bankruptcy is a procedure not for forgiving obligations but for seizing a defaulter's assets. The absence of this procedure for countries, far from being a bull point, totally falsifies Mr Wriston's thesis. The Florentine bankers had a little local difficulty in recovering their money from the English King Edward III in 1327: two bankers failed.[5] To this day, the state of Mississippi is in default on debt which it repudiated in 1875. More relevantly, few of the bonds which the South American governments failed to service in the 1930s were ever paid back at par.

The appealing parallel between the Third World debt of today and the US government Treasury bill is equally flawed. The US government is, of course, able to maintain confidence that it will repay its obligations and thus does not have any problems with rolling over its debt.

The central reason why the United States is able to maintain confidence is because its obligations are overwhelmingly denominated in its own currency, and it can print or tax as many dollars as it requires to meet its obligations. It is therefore not dependent on creating an export surplus to service its debt. Brazil would not have much problem in persuading the banks that it too would be able to meet cruzeiro debt. It can tax its own people, and if that is inconvenient, it can print cruzeiros. (This crucial distinction between foreign-currency and home-currency debt is the main reason why the much blazoned size of the United States' debt to foreigners is a matter of far less concern than Third World foreign-currency debt: the servicing of US debt may require inflationary American policies, and the size of foreigners' holdings of dollar assets may provoke a serious weakening of confidence in its value and a run on the currency. But the United States will never be obliged to default on Federal debt.)

Walter Wriston was far from a lone voice. There was further

support for the doctrine of sovereign loan safety, which was that the Western authorities would finally stand behind any debtor, or creditor, which got into trouble. Nothing like an 'official guarantee' could be deduced explicitly from the statements of Western public figures, but there is no doubt that the encouragement of the recycling of OPEC surpluses by the world's leading monetary authorities appeared to corroborate this assumption of the bankers. Offical concern focused only on the fearful consequences for world trade and political stability if the lending did not occur and the purchasing power of the Third World were to be suddenly diminished. This concern was quite right and proper but should have been supplemented by a second: an intelligent anxiety about the character and sustainability of this process of commercial lending.

In effect, Western policy-makers ran away from the problem while enthusiastically cheering from the sidelines the banking system's attempt to deal with it. The joy of bank lending was that it fulfilled the purposes of policy-makers while absolving them, at least temporarily, from the need to spend any public money, increase any public deficits or even set in place the framework which could have rendered the process safe. The soft option reigned supreme.

Thus Mr Johannes Witteveen, de Larosière's predecessor as managing director of the IMF, explicitly encouraged the development of the Euro-markets in the wake of the 1973–4 oil shock:

These countries have to do something with their foreign-exchange receipts. If they do not spend them on imports, they have to hold them in financial claims, which are forms of lending. Unavoidably, therefore, the overall current account surplus of the oil-exporting countries generates a capital flow of the same magnitude to the oil-importing countries. The key question is how to ensure that the pattern of such flows helps rather than hinders the achievement of monetary and economic stability . . . Private markets have a basic role to play here, and it is to them that we must look for the main contribution in financing prospective balance-of-payments disequilibria. In the first instance, the Euro-currency markets may be expected to be the main channel. These markets are well equipped to handle large volumes of funds, and they offer the flexibility and the anonymity that the lenders desire.[6]

By December 1976 Mr Witteveen was praising the 'very useful function overall' which the banking system had fulfilled. In

May 1977 he said: 'By and large these banking systems have done a commendable job in recycling the surpluses of the OPEC countries in a manner that has helped to sustain world trade and economic activity.'

The managing director of the Fund was merely expressing the sentiments of the advanced countries which dominate the IMF. Mr Denis Healey, then Britain's Chancellor of the Exchequer, told the Fund's annual meeting in September 1977: 'The commercial banking system has rightly played the main role in financing these deficits until now and has shown immense resourcefulness in doing so.' His Conservative successor, Sir Geoffrey Howe, speaking at the IMF meeting in September 1979, said: 'Meantime we must all hope that flows from the private sector to many LDCs [less developed countries] will continue to grow. These should include not only lending for development through the private banking system but also a much wider range of private investment from the industrial countries.'[7] Similarly, US Secretary of the Treasury Mr G. William Miller gave encouragement at the 1979 IMF meeting: 'We all recognize that the private markets will, in the future as in the past, have to play by far the major role in channelling financing from surplus to deficit nations.'

This was a policy which commanded wide assent among the advanced countries and, indeed, was endorsed at the highest levels of policy-making. At the Tokyo summit of the seven leaders of the biggest market economies in June 1979, the communiqué which was issued on behalf of all participants, including the British Prime Minister, Mrs Margaret Thatcher, could hardly have been more explicit:

The latest decision substantially to increase oil prices will also severely increase the problems facing developing countries without oil resources as well as the difficulties for developed countries in helping them. The decision could even have a crippling effect on some of the developing countries. In this situation, we recognize, in particular, the need for the flow of financial resources to the developing countries to increase, including private and public, bilateral and multilateral resources.[8]

Even as late as the autumn of 1981, only nine months before the Mexican crunch, Sir Geoffrey Howe once again praised the virtues of the private banks:

The private markets have also served us well in the continued success of the recycling process ... the success of both newly industrializing and middle-income countries in attracting private capital, particularly bank lending, reflects their ability to offer opportunities for profitable and productive investment. This has enabled them to finance their external payments and to raise their living standards and is surely the best form of recycling.

Official statements from the most authoritative sources could also give quite specific and detailed endorsement to the level of bank lending. Thus Mr Paul Volcker, the chairman of the US Federal Reserve, argued in a speech in March 1980:

The impression I get from the data I have reviewed is that the recycling process has not yet pushed exposure of either borrowers or lenders to an unsustainable point in the aggregate, especially for American banks, whose share in total bank lending to non-oil developing countries in recent years has declined and whose share of claims on those countries in total assets has also declined. But problem cases exist now and will no doubt continue to show up.[9]

Implicitly, the advanced-country policy-makers waved aside the problems of the late 1970s – the Turkeys and Zaïres – as small and temporary ones. International bank lending was the subject of a symphony of official suasion. Would that the present views of the same policy-makers were consistent with their previous statements in demanding an end to negative transfers instead of insisting on them. All these gentlemen, and one lady, appear to have no doubt about their credentials in now urging the debtors to tighten their belts in an effort to service debt, a position which is exactly the contrary of their previous stance.

The belief that sovereign debtors would honour their obligations was pervasive throughout the 1970s in the Euro-markets and was responsible for some curious notions. Lending to Eastern Europe, for example, was said to be sanctified by the Soviet guarantee, or 'umbrella': the Russians would not harm their own creditworthiness by allowing their satellites to fall behind on payments. Nevertheless, Poland did exactly that in 1981.

Later in the 1970s the banks began to develop more elaborate techniques which, they claimed, could better assess country risk, though they hardly made much impact on the terms offered to borrowers. In 1979, for example, the spreads (the margins) paid over the cost of funds to the banks by Argentina and Mexico were just under 1 per cent, by Poland 1 per cent, by Hungary and France just over ½ per cent and by Sweden ½ per cent. It is difficult to justify the narrowness of these spreads on any theory other than that sovereign borrowers never default. How else could France's debt seriously pay only ¼ per cent less than Argentina's?[10] Spreads did not genuinely reflect risk and could not do so without becoming so large as to stop the lending. When reality crowded in and confidence failed, the response was not the widening of spreads but a halt to the lending. The tiny differentials between these borrowing countries were a mere pretence at risk measurement.

Where the borrowers were fairly well known and could be assigned straight credit risks, it became the practice to accept parts of syndicated loans over the telex: if the big banks were leading a syndicate, the small banks did not want to be left out for fear that they would not have the opportunity when a syndication was next on offer from the same source. The lead banks in a syndicate stood to gain substantial arrangement fees, and the touting for Third World business became a sophisticated *affaire*; a successful deal often culminated in lavish entertainment of the respective parties at some suitably modest hostelry like the Ritz or Claridges. Syndicated lending had its own social milieu: the successful young international banker was invited to the right parties and had his bank's name on the right tombstones, the ubiquitous lists of bank names published in the financial press that acted as the outward record of the previous month's lending. During most of the 1970s international lending was where the brightest staff of the banks headed. It was where the apparent profits were, and the air tickets and hotel rooms were thrown in too. No one wanted to be left out.

Immense effort went into selling loans to the Third World. If there was no risk that a country would fail to repay, and if in addition any loan was automatically profitable by virtue of its specification of a margin over the cost of funds, it followed that the way to become bigger and better and more profitable was to sign up as many sovereign debtors as possible. The City press even kept a league table of which bank had succeeded in syndicating most. Every self-respecting banker strove to be at the head of it. Banks from every country joined in the lending, even when they had to borrow dollars to do it and when, for this reason, their own central banks were unable to act as effective lenders of last resort.

The increasing size of the banks' organizations, and the habit of revolving foreign postings fairly rapidly, also put a premium on speedy (if not always sensible) results. An American and a French bank opened representative offices in Gabon in the mid-1970s and expected profits within twelve months. The result was $600 million in officially guaranteed export credits and $679 million in syndicated loans. The other results were a triumphal highway linking the airport and the presidential palace, a hotel sector with occupancy rates resembling those of a seaside resort in mid-winter, a fleet of commercial jet aircraft, enlarged government buildings and one of the world's least economic railways, built against the World Bank's planning advice.[11] If you believed sovereign debt was safe, the uses of the funds were of no importance. Managers were measured by short-term results: the more loans the better. In a 'hardship posting' like Gabon, they could count on being out within two years.

The polite reason given by governments for why the snowball went on rolling for so long is that they did not have the information by which to assess the full extent of the indebtedness of some of the major borrowers, a position in theory to be rectified by the bank-backed Institute for International Finance in Washington, created after the debt crisis. The publication of figures assembled by the BIS on the commercial banks' exposure to individual countries has now been speeded up but at the time appeared only after a time lag of six months. The evidence on the shorter maturities of the debt of many of the problem countries, which would have provided some early indication of the difficulty they were having in raising medium- and long-term credits, still appears only some six months after the event. But the reality is that the failure of the credit market was due to more than merely a lack of information. The very structure of the syndicated credit encouraged the uncritical herd instinct. When other people in the market had confidence in the debtors, your bank's debt could always be refinanced if you wanted to get out, so that there was no need to get out. Not only did the old debt get rolled over but the interest on the old debt was met by new debt, and the new debt, in addition, provided a net resource flow to the favoured Third World countries throughout the 1970s.

For those with eyes to see, the first signs of ebbing confidence in the accelerating pace of international bank lending were the shortening of maturities on debt that was being rolled over and the steady build-up of short-term debt with a maturity of less than one year in many of the major debtors before 1982. By tradition, the device of shortening the term of loans is meant to make the lending bank's position safer because the loans are locked into risk for a shorter time. However, the collective effect of the entire system's shortening of its maturities is to bring forward the day of reckoning. As medium- and long-term debt became more difficult to find, some of the largest debtors drew down their reserves to redeem maturing debt. They then drew down their short-term credit arrangements, but the net result was to leave an even larger sum to be redeemed within the year.

By 1982 the pace of new lending was hectic. Mexico borrowed $6.4 billion in the six months before the August crunch,[12] an increase in the US banks' exposure that ran at an annual rate of 34 per cent.[13] But the credits coming up for redemption were even greater, until eventually a liquidity gap opened up, and Mexico was unable to redeem due debt. As with other examples of financial cycles, the process of euphoria and over-trading had given way to hesitation – characterized in Minsky's theory of financial instability as 'distress' – and ultimately to revulsion.[14]

As the stampede went into reverse and new credit dried up, the very mechanisms which had been introduced to assure individual banks of the lack of risk were revealed as making the system as a whole more unstable. Variable interest rates shifted the risk of interest-rate changes to borrowers, but it merely diverted attention from the real risk, which lay in the soundness of the borrowing itself. The floating-rate structure in turn hastened the advent of incredibility. The syndicated loan, which had seemed to protect an individual bank from excessive exposure to any one country, instead ensured that the system as a whole was exposed. The cross-default clauses in every loan agreement, designed to assure creditors that they would not be placed behind others in the queue for repayment by giving them the right to call simultaneous default on their loans if others called default, put *every* bank at the mercy of *any* bank insisting on immediate repayment. The shortening of maturities that were anyway far shorter than traditional official balance-of-payments financing ensured that the two blades of the liquidity scissors – mounting repayments combined with falling reserves and short-term credit – snapped shut with breathtaking speed.

An unsupported and insufficiently regulated banking system was revealed, in the period 1979–82, to be an inherently unstable source of balance-of-payments funding for the developing world. When times were good, the banks thrust tempting loans on to favoured Third World governments, though they were in no position to ensure that sound economic policies would be pursued. When times turned bad, the banks were no longer prepared to fund mounting deficits.

The irony is that, with some clear exceptions, the private financing of Third World current-account deficits over the decade to 1982 was a considerable success story from the point of view of world growth and public policy. Neither the level of the debt nor its results need have caused alarm: the problem lay not so much in the amounts of money which were extended but in the nature of the lending. The debt, after all, did allow the non-oil developing countries to maintain far higher growth rates than they would otherwise have been able to do. Comparing the pre-1973 and post-1973 period, we know that industrial-country growth slowed down markedly: the surprise is that the non-oil developing countries managed to compensate for this slow-down to a large degree in their main markets and the rise in the cost of their main imports by making up their import capacity with debt. Indeed, the average annual rate of growth of the non-oil Third World between 1973 and 1981 was 5.1 per cent, compared with 5.8 per cent in the period 1967–72.[15] In retrospect this was a quite remarkable performance. The industrial countries, by contrast, slowed down from an annual average growth of 4.4 per cent in 1967–72 to one of 2.8 per cent. If the developing world had slowed down still more, it would have cut its imports from the industrial countries and hence their growth. From the world's point of view, it was better for the lending to have taken place clumsily than not at all.

One cost, of course, was a rising debt burden for the debtors, though on conventional measures it looked far from unsustainable even at the end of the decade. The real value of total debt for the non-oil developing countries, expressed in constant 1975 dollars, rose from $169 billion in 1973 to $294.7 billion in 1979.[16] But even this rise went side by side with a substantial expansion in the Third World's foreign-currency earnings. The total debt to export ratio was 115.4 per cent in 1973 and rose to 130.2 per cent in 1978. But the following year it was back to

119.2 per cent, scarcely higher than at the beginning of the decade. The debt service to export ratio – the amount of interest payments and repayments of principal due in a year relative to exports – indicated a slightly graver problem: it rose from 15.9 per cent in 1973 to 19 per cent in 1979. If, however, the debt had been contracted at maturities longer than the typical eight-year loan, even this ratio could have been contained at more or less its level at the beginning of the decade. Clearly, the conventional debt ratios tell us little about the likelihood of crisis.

The truth is that neither conventional creditworthiness indicators nor the results of Third World policies suggest that the build-up of debt, at least to the end of the 1970s, was misplaced. What *was* unsustainable was the system and nature of that debt. The similarity of the conventional creditworthiness ratios at the beginning and the end of the period merely disguise a much more fundamental change in the structure of the outstanding debt.

The advanced countries had thrown a single vulnerable section of their economies, the banking system, into a task which it could not bear without official support. The key difference between the position of the Third World debtors in 1973 and at the end of the 1970s was that their debt was no longer largely official debt: it was commercial debt to the banks. Governments can afford to roll over interest and capital obligations as circumstances require. Banks cannot without embroiling themselves in a dynamic of increasing incredibility. The share of outstanding commercial debt in total loans rose from 11.6 per cent in 1973 to 37.5 per cent in 1982.[17] In the case of the richer debtors in Latin America the proportion rose from 23.8 per cent to 62 per cent. The debtors inevitably became vulnerable to the disintegration of market confidence. The sharp rise in bank debt would itself have eventually been enough to cause the lending to stop. External shocks such as the rise in interest rates merely accelerated the process. Unsupported private banks could never have provided enough time for the debtors to repay by generating export surpluses. There was no contemplation of this until the smooth, automatic new lending which had been expected failed to arrive.

The banks were simply unable to maintain their own confidence in the commercial nature of the loans they were making, with the result that the mechanism of the commercial banks' balance-of-payments financing became in 1982 the very opposite of what had been intended. The international credit market had been justified on the grounds that countries should have time to 'put their own houses in order', but it instead became a burden on developing countries already facing, in the commodity markets, a magnified impact of the industrial world's gathering recession. It acted to exacerbate the depressive forces in the world economy rather than to alleviate them. The unregulated international credit market had failed.

5

A CRITIQUE OF THE IMF'S 'SOLUTION'

Being an optimist, I don't assume it to be
inevitable when I'm asked to jump out of the frying pan
that I'll land in the fire – but I worry.

GEORGE J. STIGLER

Like the captains of ships, central bankers and finance ministers are duty-bound to proclaim that their charge is not about to sink, if only to avoid panic. The reality, though, is not always so comforting. Many of them had been seriously afraid, as the debt crisis broke with a vengeance in the summer of 1982, of what Mr Jacques de Larosière, the managing director of the IMF, called in retrospect 'a real threat to the integrity of the international financial and trading system'.[1] On this matter Mr de Larosière presented accurately – and continues to do so – the consensus view of the advanced countries' governments and monetary authorities. Their mood began to change only as the IMF gradually put its 'adjustment programmes' in place and as the debtor countries exhibited a remarkable willingness to accept cuts in output and living standards in order to realize foreign exchange for debt service. It looked as if the world was receding from the abyss.

By June 1984 Mr de Larosière was proclaiming that the pessimists had been proved wrong. The resolution of the debt problem, he said, 'can be viewed today with greater confidence than a year ago, in spite of some important difficulties which need to be tackled'. He said that, overall, the banks had made new money available to the developing countries to ease the speed at which they were required to generate debt-service dollars, while the countries themselves had 'continued to address the root causes of their financial difficulties' under Fund supervision.

Most crucially, perhaps, the Fund's managing director claimed that the official approach, as it is presently constituted, was sustainable in the medium term. In a speech in Stockholm in February 1985, for example, Mr de Larosière said:

Despite the progress achieved thus far in handling the debt problems, there are some who question the ability of the indebted countries to cope with the burden of debt-servicing over the medium term. In the Fund we have examined this question very carefully. And we have concluded that, on the basis of plausible assumptions concerning policies in the debtor countries, international financing and the evolution of the world economy – including the critical assumption that trade restrictions are not intensified – a workable outcome is, indeed, possible.[2]

Perhaps a working outcome is on the borders of possibility. It is worth noting, however, that even the official as well placed as anyone to make a judgement does not commit himself to the view that a workable outcome is likely or probable. It is merely possible. The real question is surely whether, given current policies, a resolution of the debt problem can be counted on and, if not, whether the risks thereby entailed are ones which any sensible policy-maker should run.

In this chapter and the next we look closely at the medium-term prospects according to the IMF's view and conclude that the position is unsustainable. There are two broad classes of concern. The first is that even if the IMF's central projection for the medium term actually transpires, it is very hard to see how a crisis can be avoided. On its own terms, the IMF case looks weak. The second, which we turn to in the next chapter, is that the Fund's relatively optimistic outlook for the world economy could only too easily prove to be an illusion.

In looking at the question of sustainability, two central issues must be borne in mind.

The first is whether the debtor countries as a group (but also individually) will continue to be able and willing to service their foreign debt with dollars. This will depend in part on the ease with which they can expand their exports and in part on the extent to which they can grow without seeing their expanding economies suck in imports which eat into debt-service dollars. But it will also depend on the likely net flow of funds to the debtor countries over the medium term. The *net* flow is crucial. When the IMF and bankers talk about extending 'new money' to debtors, it is new money only in the sense that it constitutes new loans for the banks. If it goes to repay old debt which is maturing or to pay interest on old debt, the reality is that the debtors are not receiving any new resources at all.

As we shall see, if there is little prospect that the debtors will actually receive new money, there is correspondingly less incentive to service old debt. The more new money is advanced to them, the greater will be their willingness to co-operate with the international financial system. The loans, in other words, are safe as long as they are met by new ones and not in reality serviced or repaid. This surprising judgement arises from a bizarre and anomalous situation. Before the debt crisis broke no one could or would have argued in these terms, for a very simple reason. They would have regarded net transfers from debtors to creditors on the scale envisaged as an aberration, as we do and (perhaps unsurprisingly) as the debtor countries do.

The second key issue is whether the amounts of money that need to be advanced to make the debt problem sustainable from the debtors' point of view are, in fact, likely to be forthcoming without a change in institutional arrangements. Will the banks or lenders be prepared to lend the extra dollars? What will be the consequences of their exposure to the debtor countries if they do? If the new money is not likely to be forthcoming from mainly private sources, it would be rash indeed to declare that the debt crisis was over. The debtors' burden of paying interest and redeeming old debt would be heavy and resented. Yet this is precisely the situation at present. The prospects for servicing future obligations, even on the most rosy view, look too fragile to justify renewed commercial lending.

The reason why there is a potential conflict between the interests of bankers and those of the developing debtors is, as we have seen, because imports are important to their growth. For any country by far and away the largest source of foreign exchange is its exports. So the first determinant of the scale of imports is the growth of exports, which in turn depends in part on the policies pursued by a country (for example, the level at which it sets its exchange rate) and in part on the growth of demand for those exports in the rest of the world. In the case of the developing economies, this means primarily the growth of demand in the industrial countries, which still accounts for nearly 70 per cent of world imports.[3] The pace of industrial-country demand affects both the likely export volume of the developing world and the price of each unit of its exports.

A country's second source of foreign exchange for the

purchase of imports is finance. This includes official credits through such institutions as the World Bank or bilateral lending by the industrial countries, outright grants or aid, direct investment by foreign companies in its plants and so forth, and portfolio investment in the shares or bonds of companies and its government. But for the major debtor countries the most important and fastest-growing source of finance over the last decade has been lending by the advanced countries' banks. Broadly, the more the banks were prepared to lend, the higher could be the imports of the developing countries they lent to and consequently the higher could be the level of output and the living standards of those countries. Thus in looking at the prospects for the sustainability of present levels of debt it is crucial to assess whether the amount that bankers are able to lend without worsening their present fragilitỹ is reconcilable with the amount that the developing countries want to borrow in order to grow. Will the debtors' growth rates be high enough to avoid social and political explosions?

In the IMF's view, there will be a gradual return to 'spontaneous' lending by the banks as the debtor countries win back their creditworthiness.[4] They will do so, according to the Fund's projections, by generating trade surpluses, and hence foreign exchange, effectively to pay back the debt. In order to establish anew the conditions for a resumption of private lending, the developing world has been subjected to what the Fund calls a 'case-by-case approach'. In reality, the approach has not been case-by-case at all but has involved similar IMF 'adjustment programmes', with four common elements, in exchange for some financing of payments deficits and the Fund's success in persuading the commercial banks to expand their lending through the rescheduling of maturing debt.

First, the IMF generally insists on a sharp cut in a government's budget deficit of spending over revenues, sometimes by as much as 10 per cent of GDP. According to the Fund's theory, this has two effects. It reduces the government's demands on domestic savings and hence helps to lower interest rates so as not to 'crowd out' investment. It thereby helps to reduce the need for foreign inflows of capital. In reality, it improves the trade balance – and thus cuts the need for balance-of-payments financing – both by reducing domestic demand, activity and imports and by ensuring that those who have the potential to export do so because the home market is depressed.

The second element is a strict limit on, and a declining growth path for, domestic credit expansion – broadly, new borrowing in the domestic currency of the country by the private sector. The objective is to control the quantity of money and thereby inflation. The reality is to add another depressive force to the economy, as interest rates have to rise, and to stay at high levels, in order to curb new borrowing.

The third common element to the programmes is a 'realistic' exchange rate – devaluation against other countries' currencies so as to make the goods of exporters and those who compete with imports more attractive in price. One consequence is a rise in the price of imports, expressed in domestic currency, and a stimulus to inflation.

The fourth common element is the pursuit of government spending cuts, often through the abandonment of subsidies and price controls on the grounds that they distort the efficient working of the markets and hence the allocation of investment and manpower to the most profitable uses.

The net result, as we have seen, is generally a severe slump, often combined with a sharp acceleration in inflation. Recession and curbs on bank lending also hit hardest at the private sector and its investment, even though the IMF rests its hopes for future economic performance on business dynamism.

In defence of Fund policies, it has been argued that the pain of the adjustment period would be even greater without IMF finance because imports would have to be cut even more rapidly. The reality, though, is that many debtors would merely have been pushed into a decisive default on their debt unless the IMF had provided some new funds and forced the banks to provide others to meet part of the debt service. In this sense, the Fund can be seen as acting as the lender of last resort to the banks, for any funds which it provides go straight back to the creditors and act as the catalyst for the debtor generating even more foreign exchange itself.

Moreover, there is no good reason why the IMF's programmes should require such rapid adjustment or should be based on such inadequate finance. A country could adjust its current-account deficit nearer to balance by gradually switching production from home to foreign markets, but Fund programmes always involve the short, sharp shock of expenditure, and hence output *cuts*, rather than merely switching. The reason is that the Fund would simply have been unable, under present policies, to finance more gradual programmes, given the number of countries which have required Fund access since 1982 and the reluctance of its dominant advanced-country members to expand its resources.

The theory, however, is that such programmes are politically sustainable because no more pain is administered after the first undeniably unpleasant crunch. The economy is said to make a once-and-for-all adjustment whereby its output and living standards are reduced in the process of carving off a part of the diminished whole to generate the foreign exchange to service debt. The economy can then begin growing again as its exports rise. As soon as some part of that export increase is under the country's belt, its imports can begin to rise in parallel.

This has two effects. First, it allows a continued trade surplus to generate the foreign exchange to continue servicing – and repaying – the debt. Secondly, it allows domestic living standards to rise gradually, though not steeply and never back on to the growth path that the economy was on before the crisis struck. Nevertheless, both living standards and unemployment should in theory gradually improve from slump levels, thus relieving social and political pressures. Eventually, the effect of continued trade surpluses would be to cut the amount of debt relative to income and exports to levels where once again, so the theory holds, the private banks will want to lend and 'normality' returns.[5] The revival of confidence would mean that it would no longer be necessary to run trade surpluses because the old money-go-round of borrowing more to service old debt and provide an additional margin could resume. The countries would therefore be able to maintain rates of growth that were rather higher but now compatible with sound borrowing.

In effect, the Fund seems to want to restore the *status quo ante* (though with better behaved debtors and more cautious bankers). It is aiming to go back to the period before the Mexican crisis of 1982 and to restore the faith of both bankers and debtors in the efficacy of free international capital markets. Given the events which have taken place since then, this is a somewhat surprising objective in itself. The *status quo ante* was deeply flawed and led inevitably to the subsequent crisis. The issue here, however, is whether Fund policies stand any chance of getting the world to go where it wants. The path appears to be strewn with forbidding obstacles.

We are a long way from such 'normality' yet, and it is by no means clear that the Fund's strategy is workable, as can be seen by looking in detail at its medium-term staff projections for the rest of the decade. The Fund's 1985 *World Economic Outlook* contains a 'baseline scenario' until 1990 for various groups of its member countries: the net oil exporters, Asian countries and so forth. This practice of grouping results together preserves the confidentiality of information provided to the Fund, but it does, of course, suffer from the considerable drawback of all averages: it fails to distinguish the cases which might prove the most troublesome, a point to which we return in Chapter 7. But a useful glimpse of the outlook, as the Fund sees it, can be provided by the exercise.

For this purpose, we look at the outlook for all the indebted developing countries taken together – 123 countries (the developing world with the exception of eight Middle Eastern oil exporters). We also look at the two IMF groupings which contain the greatest potential for trouble in reconciling bankers and debtors: the seven major borrowers and the western hemisphere. The seven major borrowers (Argentina, Brazil, Indonesia, South Korea, Mexico, Philippines and Venezuela) accounted for 44 per cent of all developing-country debt in 1984. Their GDP, however, accounted for only 28 per cent of the Third World total and their exports for only 18 per cent in 1980. The thirty-three debtor countries in the western hemisphere, which include four of the seven in the previous category, accounted for 42 per cent of Third World debt in 1984, compared with 28 per cent of GDP and 16.5 per cent of exports. We also assume, for the purposes of the present argument, that the broad world picture painted by the Fund's baseline scenario holds true, though we shall return to some of its risks and uncertainties in the next chapter. Thus we are merely looking to see whether the outlook which the Fund projects is, in its own terms, internally consistent. Can the various parties in this drama indeed behave as the IMF has scripted them to? Is the amount which the Fund predicts will be lent compatible with the ultimate safety of the banking system? Is it also compatible with growth in the debtor countries high enough to make them willing to continue to service their debt?

The first point is that the Fund clearly does not see the developing world even resuming the rates of growth of the late 1960s and early 1970s, despite the drop in the *level* of output in many developing countries during the crisis of 1982 and thereafter, and despite the fact that the debtors were not overburdened with delighted populations even before the crisis hit. For the debtor countries as a whole, the IMF projects that the average annual growth of real GDP (output) will be 4.7 per cent between 1985 and 1990 compared with 6.3 per cent between 1968 and 1972 or 5.4 per cent between 1973 and 1980.

The situation for the more indebted groups of countries is worse. In the IMF's western hemisphere group, where real GDP fell by more than 4 per cent between 1981 and 1983, the average rate of growth is expected to be 4 per cent to the end of the decade compared with 6.7 per cent in 1968–72 and 5.6 per cent in 1973–80. In other words, the debtors will never regain even the growth trend – albeit from a lower base – that they had before the crisis. Far from seeing a once-and-for-all set reduction in output to service debt, followed by a resumption of the previous growth path in parallel to, though at a lower level than, the old one, the two growth paths will continue to diverge. Even on the IMF's baseline scenario, the debt crisis will continue to exert a powerful influence over the debtors' economic performance.

One reason for this projected slower growth is that investment has declined. It formed 25.5 per cent of developing-country GDP in each year from 1977 to 1981. In 1982 it began to fall and reached 21.5 per cent in 1984. In the western hemisphere the decline was sharper. Investment averaged 23.3 per cent of GDP between 1977 and 1981 and fell to 17.1 per cent in 1984, according to the IMF's figures.

To European and even American eyes, average rates of growth of around 4 per cent look fairly respectable. But they must be put in a developing-world context of high rates of population growth by comparison with stable, and in some cases declining, population in industrial countries. In addition, the growth rates of GDP need to exceed the sum of the growth of productivity (or output per person employed) and of the labour force if any impact on unemployment or under-employment in rural areas is to make itself felt. As Professor Dornbusch has pointed out, some of the medium-sized debtors in Latin America probably need 5–6 per cent annual GDP growth merely to stay ahead of labour-force growth of 3 per cent a year and productivity growth of 2–3 per cent a year.[6] Indeed, the central estimate of the Inter-American Development Bank (IADB), in its recent forecasting exercise on the prospects for debt and growth in the whole region, assumed that a 5.4 per cent annual growth rate was required over the period 1985–90 merely to stop higher unemployment.[7] Some of the largest debtors required even higher rates of growth because of more rapidly expanding labour forces. The IADB projections, for example, require growth of 6 per cent a year on average in Brazil.

The lack of reliable data for jobs, unemployment and productivity in the developing countries – even the middle-income ones like Brazil and Mexico – makes such guesses hazardous. But it is noticeable that the United Nations Economic Commission for Latin America (UNECLA) shows that urban unemployment rose in 1984 in Bolivia, Brazil, Colombia, Nicaragua, Peru and Venezuela.[8] In Brazil UNECLA puts real GDP growth at 3.5 per cent in 1984, but the rate of unemployment in the major urban areas rose by 0.75 per cent between 1983 and 1984. Partly as a result, there is little sign of any easing of the social pressures for more rapid expansion.

Measures of living standards are no more encouraging. The IADB assumes that a growth rate of GDP of 2.7 per cent a year would be required merely to stabilize GDP per head, due to natural population growth. The population growth figure implied by recent UNECLA statistics for the region is slightly lower, at 2.3 per cent a year. Taking the UNECLA figure in order to reach a cautious estimate, it is possible to calculate what the IMF's projections mean for real GDP per head in the region. On the Fund's baseline scenario, the Latin Americans will finally recover the 1980 level of output per head in 1989.

Even this modest increase is not available to improve the standard of life because a higher share of that GDP will probably have to go in earning foreign exchange to service dollar debt rather than being absorbed by domestic uses and higher living standards. Thus domestic absorption of resources

– broadly, consumption by residents of the countries concerned – fell back gently once again in 1984, despite a marginally *positive* growth of real GDP per head in Latin America of 0.2 per cent in 1983. In 1984 this measure of living standards was fully 12.9 per cent below its peak in 1980.[9] In sum, the growth performance which the IMF expects of the debtors is unlikely to make the burden of large net transfers of funds from debtors to creditors any more willingly borne.

As we have seen, the negative flow of funds from the poor countries to the rich ones is in defiance of good economics of whatever school of thought. On a classical view, the developing countries should attract capital from the industrial world because they are able to increase output more for a given increase in investment. Alternatively, the debtors need balance-of-payments finance because their domestic economies are capable of expanding more rapidly than they are able to increase their foreign-exchange earnings and imports, mainly because of their reliance on export commodities, whose demand grows less rapidly than world income. Nor do such negative transfers immediately appeal to our sense of equity. However, the question here is the more limited one of whether it is actually realistic to expect the debtors to make such transfers (rather than default on their obligations) when all the pressures are for higher growth and thus, inevitably, more imports and smaller transfers.

Certainly, a perverse flow for a few years might be something that the debtor countries would live with in the hope and expectation that larger and more prolonged transfers in the opposite direction would subsequently resume. That hope, indeed, is one of the main reasons why the debtors continue to co-operate with IMF programmes. But the most surprising element of the IMF's projections is that the negative transfer is expected to continue throughout the forecast period (i.e. until 1990) and that in the case of the large debtors it is expected to remain very considerable. There could hardly be a more clear-cut incitement to default than the combination of disappointing growth and enormous perverse transfers.

Table 4 is derived entirely from the published figures in the IMF's medium-term projection, and it spells out what happens to net debt transfers – the balance between the interest and repayments of old debt paid out by the debtors and the 'new

Table 4   Implications (ratios, percentages of exports of goods and
services) of the IMF projections, 1985 ($ billion)

	1982	1983	1984	1985	1986	1988	1990
INDEBTED DEVELOPING COUNTRIES (123)							
Total debt	747.0	790.7	827.7	865.3	896.5	986.2	1,089.9
Debt service	123.9	111.1	123.1	134.5	139.4	199.2	207.5
Interest (A)	72.3	67.4	71.0	74.0	72.5	83.5	87.0
Net new borrowing (B)	86.5	43.7	37.0	37.6	31.2	45.9	53.0
Transfer (B–A)	14.2	– 23.7	– 34.0	– 36.4	– 41.3	– 37.6	– 34.0
Vulnerability ratio (A ÷ B)	0.8	1.5	1.9	2.0	2.3	1.8	1.6
Transfer as percentage of exports	2.8%	– 4.7%	– 6.2%	– 6.2%	– 6.5%	– 4.7%	– 3.4%
MAJOR BORROWERS (7 countries)[1]							
Total debt	336.4	351.0	360.2	369.3	377.4	385.1	374.3
Debt service	61.8	49.3	53.5	57.3	59.5	87.0	82.0
Interest (A)	38.9	35.7	37.9	38.3	36.3	37.3	34.5
Net new borrowing (B)	46.2	14.6	9.2	9.1	8.1	3.9	– 5.4
Transfer (B–A)	7.3	– 21.1	– 28.7	– 29.2	– 28.2	– 33.4	– 39.9
Vulnerability ratio (A ÷ B)	0.8	2.4	4.1	4.2	4.5	9.6	—[2]
Transfer as percentage of exports	5.2%	– 15.3%	– 18.8%	– 17.9%	– 16%	– 15.5%	– 16%
WESTERN HEMISPHERE (33 countries)[3]							
Total debt	325.3	338.9	351.1	357.1	363.6	376.4	409.9
Debt service	62.0	47.3	49.4	53.7	56.5	92.4	93.8
Interest (A)	38.9	35.1	36.2	36.7	35.2	37.3	38.5
Net new borrowing (B)	41	13.6	12.2	6.0	6.5	6.5	17.1
Transfer (B–A)	2.1	– 21.5	– 24.0	– 30.7	– 28.7	– 30.8	– 21.4
Vulnerability ratio (A ÷ B)	0.9	2.6	3.0	6.1	5.4	5.7	2.3
Transfer as percentage of exports	1.7%	– 18.7%	– 19.1%	– 23.2%	– 20.3%	– 17.4%	– 9.2%

Notes: [1] Major borrowers are Argentina, Brazil, Indonesia, South Korea, Mexico, Philippines and Venezuela (44 per cent of LDC debt in 1984). [2] Theoretically infinite. [3] Forty-two per cent of LDC debt in 1984.

Source: Authors' calculations derived from IMF, World Economic Outlook, Washington DC, April 1985. For data until 1986, see Tables 36, 45, 46 and 49. After 1986, see Table 51 (for the implied totals of exports of goods and services) and Table 52 (for debt, debt service and interest payments as a share of exports of goods and services). Because of roundings in the IMF's figures, the actual values in this table derived from those figures should not be taken as more than a general indication of the IMF's projections.

money' received from the banks. (This excludes the net flow resulting from new direct investment by companies less repatriated profits and dividends, concentrating on the most important, controversial and variable element of the total net flow.) Even in the crisis year of 1982 the broad group of indebted developing countries received $14 billion more in new credits than they were required to pay out. This was not a large positive transfer, amounting to only 2.8 per cent of the debtor countries' exports, and it was low by the standards of the previous decade. But the direction was at least correct. Clearly, these countries still had the most obvious incentive to continue to service their debts because the banks and other creditors lent them more than enough money to pay their interest bills. By 1983, the transfer had turned negative to the tune of $23.7 billion, or 4.7 per cent of their exports of goods and services. In 1984 the negative transfer rose again to 6.2 per cent of exports, and the projection is that it will peak at 6.5 per cent of exports in 1986 before gradually receding to 3.4 per cent of exports at the end of the decade. Politically, though, that is little consolation. Not only are the largest transfers still to come, but they will continue with no prospect of remission even on a scenario which the IMF regards as favourable.

Those figures, moreover, apply to the broad group of all debtors: the predicament of the seven major borrowers and the western hemisphere countries is even more difficult. For the big seven, the negative transfer is 18.8 per cent of their exports in 1984, from which point it declines gently to 15.0 per cent in 1988 before *rising* again to 16.0 per cent in 1990. In the case of the western hemisphere, the negative transfer peaks at 23.2 per cent of exports in 1985 before gently declining to 17.4 per cent in 1988, and then a sharper fall to 9.2 per cent at the end of the decade is projected. (This sharp decline at the end of the period will come about only if the IMF is right to assume, without explanation, that total lending will increase by 4.4 per cent a year between 1988 and 1990 compared with only 1.7 per cent a year between 1986 and 1988.)

Table 4 also shows an indicator called the 'vulnerability ratio', a concept usefully coined by Anatole Kaletsky to provide a quick reference point to a country's temptation to default on, or repudiate, its debts.[10] This ratio of new borrowing (over and above any repayments) to interest payments is below 1 when there is a positive or normal transfer of funds to the debtor countries, so that they have no incentive to do other than service their debt. The larger the negative transfer, the greater the temptation to examine seriously the options of suspending debt service and the higher the 'vulnerability ratio'. In other words, the IMF's projection that new lending is sharply less than debt service is a danger signal. In the case of the seven major borrowers, interest payments are expected to exceed net new borrowing by a factor of more than nine in 1988 and even more thereafter. The western hemisphere group looks scarcely more encouraging. Interest payments exceed net new borrowing by a factor of around six even in 1988.

Clearly, there is a reasonable prospect, on these figures, that the rescheduling negotiations, which seem most likely just to hold to the necessary *increase* in total bank lending, will offer some unpleasant excitements. Any such prospect of large and continuing negative transfers appears to us to be wholly implausible, not least because of the background of disappointing growth rates. But let us continue drawing out the implications of the I M F's 'most likely' outlook by assuming, for the sake of argument, that all of these debtor countries will behave themselves exactly as predicted by the Fund. They will decide, by hook or by crook, to keep their side of the bargain, to run substantial trade surpluses and to forgo all the opportunities that these would otherwise provide for a faster growth rate and higher living standards. They will do so, moreover, for the rest of the decade in order to meet their obligations to pay bank interest. They may do all this, but will the banks keep their side of the bargain? Is the outlook for bank lending any more plausible than the outlook for prompt payment of present commitments by debtor countries?

For the group of western hemisphere countries the total of outstanding debt is expected to grow at a compound rate of 2.6 per cent a year between 1984 and 1990. For the major debtors total debt will grow by 1.7 per cent a year to 1988 and will then decline over the period to 1990, so that the projected compound rate for the whole period is a low 0.6 per cent. These figures refer to total debt, including official debt. But we know from the Fund's analysis that it expects little or no increase in official lending, so it seems fair to assume that the Fund is projecting a rather more rapid increase in bank debt. Even if bank debt were to grow in line with total debt, it is clear that the banks' exposure will continue to grow in money terms, despite the maturity of much of the outstanding debt. The reschedulings which have taken place so far in theory oblige the western hemisphere debtors to repay some $100 billion of principal in 1987 and 1988 in addition to their interest payments. But these maturity dates have aroused not the serious expectation that money will actually change hands but merely the surmise that there will be further hard bargaining about another postponement and, with it, the headache of keeping the smaller banks in line with present

Table 5   Implications of IMF projections for the exposure of the nine US money-centre banks ($ billion)

	EXPOSURE IN 1984	EXPOSURE AS PERCENTAGE OF CAPITAL IN 1984	EXPOSURE IN 1990[1]	EXPOSURE AS PERCENTAGE OF CAPITAL IN 1990
Argentina	5,270	15.4	5,481	10.8
Brazil	15,397	44.9	16,013	31.5
Indonesia	2,871	8.4	2,986	5.9
South Korea	5,874	17.1	6,109	12.0
Mexico	14,553	42.4	15,135	29.8
Philippines	3,868	11.3	4,023	7.9
Venezuela	7,456	21.7	7,754	15.3
Total	55,289	161	57,501	113

Note: [1] IMF projections show the total debt of seven major borrowers rising by 4 per cent between 1984 and 1990. The total capital of nine money-centre banks (Bank of America, Citibank, Chemical, Chase Manhattan, Morgan Guaranty Trust, Manufacturers Hanover, Continental Illinois, Bankers Trust and First National Bank of Chicago) was $34.3 billion as of 30 September 1984. The growth of capital, recently high under regulatory pressure, is assumed to be 6.8 per cent, in line with the IMF's projected annual growth of nominal GDP in the industrial countries. Capital in 1990 is thus assumed to be $50.84 billion. The figures for 1984 are from Salomon Bros., Inc., *A Review of Bank Performance*, New York, 1985, Figure 54, p. 79.

arrangements. It is new worries rather than new cash which the banks now expect from these maturity dates, as the IMF implicitly admits by showing that total debt will continue to rise.

The implication, therefore, is that the process of reschedulings and IMF oversight of domestic policies in the major debtor countries will have to continue if this operation is to be repeated. That, of course, will raise tricky political problems in the debtor countries. But it will also create problems among the banks. If the big banks have to take over a part of the small banks' exposures, the problem for the big banks will become still more acute. However, that problem is not taken into account in Table 5, which assumes that the big banks will increase their exposures in line with the IMF's overall projection of the increase in the debtors' total outstanding debt. As the table shows, the IMF projections for 1990 suggest that the spectre of debtor power over the nine money-centre banks will not have been banished entirely even by the end of the decade.

The calculations in the table assume, as a central estimate, that the capital of the banks will rise roughly in line with the size of the advanced economies, having increased much more rapidly over the previous five years under pressure from official bank regulators. Even if these capital increases were indeed what they seem – and they are not, as we shall see – then the exposures of the money-centre banks to the major debtors, though lower, would still be dangerous by the end of the decade. It would still take only a default by Argentina, Mexico and Brazil to wipe out more than two-thirds of their primary capital. The serious threat of any such thing would still be enough to provoke a devastating run on the deposits of the major banks.

There is an additional problem – namely, the quality of much of the apparent increase in bank capital. Although the recent increases have been large – amounting, in the case of the big American banks, to about one-fifth in 1984, for example – they have generally taken the form of long-term loans rather than equity capital. Thus they have still to be serviced, unlike shares whose dividends are subject to the bank's profitability. Although the loans do provide a cushion for the bank in the event of a total liquidation, when they would be available to pay depositors, this is unlikely to be of much consolation in other circumstances. Any prospect of a default by the banks on due service of their new capital would be disastrous for the confidence of their depositors. Moreover, one respected City of London analyst has pointed out that many of the new loans thereby raised have been from other banks rather than the public at large.[11] If this is the case, the banks will have only temporarily created the illusion that their capital position is sounder, while leaving the banking system as a whole as interlockingly exposed as before.

The IMF's projections for the increase in the exposures of all 123 indebted developing countries, rather than just the major debtors, seem even more over-optimistic. The compound growth rate of total debt is assumed to be 4.7 per cent a year between 1984 and 1990, implying a real rise in exposures of nearly 2 per cent a year after allowing for industrial-country inflation. The total debt of the developing countries rises from $827.7 billion in 1984 to $1,089.9 billion in 1990. Overall, the West's commercial banks are projected to end the decade with more developing-country debt on their books in real terms than they had immediately prior to the 1982 crisis, and the exposure relative to their capital base will have declined only marginally, and certainly not to the point at which the banks could look with equanimity on the prospect of a unilateral suspension of debt service by the debtors. In no meaningful sense, from a banker's point of view, would the debt crisis have been resolved.

This unrewarding prospect, moreover, was posited on the assumption that the debtor countries – especially the major debtors with individual 'debtor power' to inflict real damage on some of the biggest banks – will behave exactly as the IMF projects. They have to behave themselves impeccably. As the Fund puts it, it is implicitly assumed that they will not lapse into 'weak policies' which will reduce their trading surpluses and their ability to service currently contracted debt. The temptation for the debtors, however, is not merely outright default, though circumstances may push them that far. The position of the banks gives them a strong incentive to threaten default unless terms far more generous than those presently offered are put on the table. As time goes on and the pressures continue to mount, the debtors will expect the banks to recognize that they are partners facing the danger of default and will expect them to bear an increasing share of the sacrifices involved in avoiding it. Both debtors' and banks' performance may be widely different from the rosy expectations of the IMF.

Some simple arithmetic shows just how problematic this could be for the banks. Additional new lending of $15 billion a year to the seven major debtors – which would still be less than half of the projected negative transfer once interest payments on the new money were added in – would leave the total debt in 1990 at $464 billion, representing a compound growth rate since 1984 of 4.3 per cent a year. If the debtors succeeded in extracting enough new lending to all but negate the perverse transfer with some $30 billion new lending each year, the compound growth rate of total debt would be 7.4 per cent, and the banks would end the decade more heavily exposed to this small group of the largest debtors than they were in 1984. Even on a basically favourable world economic outlook, the banks would be more deeply enmeshed in the debt crisis than they were when it broke at the beginning of the decade.

The very difficulty of reconciling the conflict of interests of bankers and debtors over the amount of credit to be extended in future has led some leading political figures in the developed world – notably Mr George Shultz, the U S Secretary of State[12] – to suggest that there may be another way out of the dilemma. The theory, which is not supported by the IMF, is that an expansion of sales of government-issued bonds or direct equity investment by Western multinationals in plant and machinery in the developing countries may help to ease the financing gap. In reality, though, the theory is no more than a forlorn hope.

Direct investment in the developing countries certainly has considerable merits. It is probably one of the most productive forms of resource flow, in that it tends to take skills and technology with it, unlike bank lending. Nevertheless, the profits and dividends which it generates are in the domestic currency of the country concerned and still require trade surpluses on its part if it is to generate the foreign exchange required to provide a commercial return to the investing company in the advanced countries. Though the illusion of a properly based commercial transaction may be maintained for longer than with commercial bank lending, and thus the inflow of investment may outstrip the outflow of profits and dividends for longer, this source can no more be guaranteed to provide sustained transfers than can bank credit. Moreover, the point at which direct investors require net transfers to them – as repatriated profits outstrip new funds – is likely to be just as arbitrary as with bank credit and may stimulate or provoke similar defaults. The only advantage, from the point of view of Western monetary authorities, is that the impact of such defaults would be dispersed widely among many advanced-country companies and bond-holders and not concentrated on the banks.

The merits of direct investment as a source of development finance are thus not overwhelming, but the hope that it might nevertheless provide some temporary respite for the banks and debtors is unrealistic. The flows of direct investment are simply not large enough. The relevant figures for the net transfer to or from the developing countries on account of new direct investment minus repatriated profits are not available, but the size of capital flows of new direct investment (without deducting profits in the other direction) indicate that it cannot be expected to fill any gap left by bank finance. Table 6 shows that over the

Table 6 Capital flows to developing countries: constant 1982 prices and exchange rates; net of capital repayments but without deducting interest, profits and dividends ($ billion)

	1970	1975	1976	1977	1978	1979	1980	1981	1982	1983
Official Development Assistance (ODA)	21.10	30.23	28.97	27.59	31.70	32.68	35.34	36.48	34.74	33.82
Bilateral	18.30	24.44	23.36	21.16	24.83	26.24	28.00	28.72	27.23	26.25
Multilateral agencies	2.79	5.78	5.61	6.43	6.88	6.44	7.34	7.76	7.51	7.54
Grants by private voluntary agencies	2.24	2.02	1.96	1.98	1.89	2.01	2.28	1.98	2.31	2.21
Non-concessional flows	28.59	51.67	54.85	58.89	65.39	53.83	55.93	68.94	60.36	63.23
Official or officially supported	10.34	15.86	19.30	20.92	21.49	18.98	23.02	21.67	21.99	19.70
Private export credits (DAC)	5.46	6.66	9.77	11.77	11.10	9.13	10.48	11.06	7.09	5.53
Official export credits (DAC)	1.54	1.81	2.01	1.92	2.54	1.79	2.32	1.97	2.66	2.11
Multilateral	1.85	3.81	3.68	3.58	3.53	4.29	4.57	5.59	6.61	7.03
Other official and private flows (DAC)	0.65	1.13	1.16	0.84	1.56	1.18	2.11	1.92	2.63	(3.02)
Other donors[1]	0.84	2.45	2.68	2.81	2.76	2.59	3.53	1.13	3.00	(2.01)
Private	18.25	35.81	35.55	37.98	43.90	34.85	32.91	47.28	38.37	44.52
Direct investment	9.63	17.11	12.04	13.08	13.26	13.85	9.93	16.87	11.86	7.84
Bank sector[2]	7.83	18.07	21.74	20.64	26.17	20.30	21.68	29.35	26.00	36.18
Bond lending	0.78	0.63	1.77	4.26	4.47	0.70	1.30	1.06	0.51	0.50
Total receipts	51.93	83.92	85.78	88.47	98.98	88.52	93.45	107.40	97.41	100.25
For Information										
ODA to developing countries and multilateral agencies, total	21.80	33.25	31.90	31.74	34.37	34.18	37.65	36.73	36.95	36.36
DAC countries	17.74	20.84	18.78	21.25	23.47	23.52	25.96	24.88	27.72	27.60
OPEC countries	1.04	9.40	8.84	8.08	9.30	7.89	9.04	8.35	5.89	5.51
CMEA and other countries	2.61	3.00	2.81	2.72	2.61	2.73	2.92	3.40	3.33	3.26
Short-term bank lending				21.30	19.45	16.51	24.51	22.53	15.00	-2.01
IMF purchases, net[3]	0.89	4.88	4.32	-0.57	-0.97	0.54	2.46	6.05	6.41	12.49

Notes: [1] Other official flows from OPEC countries, Luxembourg (up to and including 1981), Spain and Yugoslavia.
[2] Excluding bond-lending and export credits extended by banks which are included under private export credits. Including loans by branches of OECD banks located in offshore centres and, for 1980, 1981 and 1982, participations of non-OECD banks in international syndicates.
[3] All purchases minus repayments including reserve tranches but excluding loans by the IMF Trust Fund included under multilateral ODA above.
  Figures concerning non-DAC member countries are based as far as possible on information released by donor countries and international organizations and completed by OECD Secretariat estimates based on other published and unpublished sources. They may therefore not comply in all respects with the norms and criteria used by DAC members in their statistical reports made directly to the OECD Secretariat.

Source: OECD, *Development Co-operation*, Paris, 1985. (The table was originally entitled 'Total net resource receipts of developing countries from all sources 1970-1983'.)

period 1975–83 the flow of direct investment (measured in the dollars of 1982 to strip out the effects of inflation) never fell below $7.8 billion a year but never rose above $17.1 billion a year: new flows would have to treble their highest peak over the last decade to cover the interest payments expected by the banks.

Bond lending has made a negligible contribution to developing countries' capital receipts, peaking at a maximum of over $4 billion in 1977 and 1978 but accounting for only $500 million in 1982 and 1983. By 1983 the bank sector accounted for 36 per cent of the total capital flows to the developing world (before deduction of interest, profits and dividends in the other direction), whereas direct investment accounted for 8 per cent and bond finance for 0.5 per cent.

Moreover, the richer the developed country, the less it has been able to rely on what the IMF calls 'non-debt-creating flows' such as direct investment and grant aid to finance its foreign currency needs. Over the five years 1977–81, for example, the seven major borrowers received net non-debt-creating flows worth $25.2 billion, while borrowing on commercial terms (other than from official sources) accounted for $162 billion of their external finance. Those, of course, were boom years for bank lending, but even in the five years 1982–86 the IMF projects that bank finance will come in at $38.2 billion compared with a virtually unchanged nominal total for non-debt-creating flows of $24.8 billion. Even to fill half the gap left by the decline of bank finance to the major borrowers over the two five-year periods, non-debt-creating flows would have to rise by a wholly unrealistic 250 per cent.[13]

Perhaps the most damning evidence against the argument that bonds and direct investment could gradually fill the role of bank lending is the fact that both sources have tended to move *with* bank lending rather than to counteract it in any way. Far from compensating for the swings in bank sentiment, they have merely compounded them, a trend which is most marked in the case of the seven major borrowers. According to the IMF, annual direct investment flows fell by 52 per cent between 1981 and 1984 – rather more sharply, indeed, than the 50 per cent fall in new external borrowing.[14] The reason is surely not hard to find: when the developing countries have the external finance (mainly, during the 1970s, from the banks) to grow quickly, their rapidly expanding markets become more attractive to direct investors. When they are constrained to grow slowly, direct investment grows slowly too. Direct investment can have no independent role in resolving the crisis of debt and growth, though its tendency to amplify funds from other sources may limit the required scale of other flows.

The correct judgement of the IMF itself is that it would not be realistic to count on direct investment as 'the principal medium for the movement of resources to the developing countries. The expansion of its role projected by the staff is therefore very moderate.'[15] Needless to say, the present atmosphere of constrained budget-making in all the major industrial countries also rules out any rise in grant aid – anyway an insignificant element in the flows to the middle-income debtors – or even in official lending. 'Even the maintenance of the present levels of official financing in real terms may prove difficult,' the Fund's 1985 *World Economic Outlook* remarks. 'Accordingly, it is hard to envisage any substantial rise in the scale of capital flows to developing countries without active utilization of private banking channels.'[16]

Yet, as we have seen, it is unlikely that the banking system will rise voluntarily to the task which the IMF has set it. Too many fingers have been burned in lending to the developing world for the commercial banks to risk, unaided, the same endeavour all over again. Whatever the IMF's view about going back to the *status quo ante*, it is far from the objective of the banks, which are looking for any reasonable opportunity to remove themselves from the uncertainties of sovereign lending to the Third World with as many of their assets intact as they can. The IMF's view of the scale of the negative transfers which the debtors will be prepared to make also seems extraordinary, since it implies that they will be prepared to forgo *ad infinitum* the growth of living standards for which their populations are pressing. The policy being pursued by the IMF and its advanced-country members is in reality a day-to-day and hand-to-mouth patchwork, with only the semblance of a medium-term strategy (and not a very good one). A workable outcome – Mr de Larosière's phrase – looks far from probable. It is more likely that the banks will not lend enough and that the debtors will not pay.

6

ECONOMIC UNCERTAINTIES AND THE GROWTH OF PROTECTIONISM

Sir, are you so grossly ignorant of human nature
not to know that a man may be very sincere
in good principles without having good practices?

SAMUEL JOHNSON

In the preceding chapter we argued that two central im-
probabilities are the willingness of the banks to lend and the
willingness of the debtors to pay even if the banks did lend
some 'new money' to limit the size of negative transfers. These
uncertainties, as we saw, exist even in an IMF scenario which
it regards as relatively favourable. In truth, they persist almost
regardless of what other assumptions are made about the performance of the world economy and debtor growth. The irre-
concilability of creditors and debtors, without a major policy
change, is inherent in the present structure of the debt. As we
shall see in this chapter, it is highly unlikely that there will be
such a combination of felicitous world events as to remove the
financial system from danger. Although much of the debt problem was caused by a rise in oil prices, a sharp fall now would
merely aggravate the predicament of the oil-exporting debtors
like Mexico. Lower interest rates might certainly help, but the
degree of aid is simply not large enough to remove the central
aberration of large negative transfers. Nor is relatively high
world growth or a fall in the dollar going to alter decisively the
worrying implications of the IMF view which we analysed in
the last chapter.

In short, there is no *deus ex machina* waiting in the wings to
rescue policy-makers from the need for a constructive attempt
to right past follies. The downside risks which could make the
conflicting arithmetic of banker and debtor interests more
alarming are only too apparent. Even a relatively buoyant
growth of world trade will leave some countries benefiting more
than others: the others may well fall by the wayside. Even a
healthy trend rate of growth of world economic activity may
disguise the habitual cycle of recovery and recession: the present

arrangements have to withstand the strains of a downturn as well as the easy ride of an American boom and a record American trade deficit. Perhaps crucially, the effective service of debt through negative transfers implies a continuing willingness on the part of the creditors to accept payment in the only way the debtors are able to make it. The debtors have to earn trade surpluses, and the creditors have to run corresponding trade deficits. In the latter part of this chapter we examine the ways in which the advanced countries themselves attempt to frustrate, through protectionism, the very process of repayment which they elsewhere extol. To doubt about whether the debtors can or will pay, we must add the further unlikelihood that the advanced countries will in fact be willing to allow the debtors to pay.

Let us look first at the sensitivity of the IMF's projections, flawed as we believe they are, to changes in its forecast of world conditions. First among these assumptions is the forecast that the industrial countries will grow at a rate of 3.1 per cent a year until 1990.[1] Industrial world growth is important to the IMF's hopes for a resolution of the crisis because of the resulting increase in demand for debtors' exports and their consequent ability to fund debt service and imports from the available foreign exchange. The IMF's assumed rate of growth is higher, for example, than the actual average growth rate of the OECD area between 1972 and 1982, which was 2.5 per cent.[2] Nevertheless, it is unlikely that the next decade will be characterized by oil or other shocks to the same extent as were the 1970s. As a central estimate it is hard to cavil at. What, though, would happen if the outcome were significantly higher or lower? On the IMF's calculations in its 1984 study, which used different groupings of countries from those of the 1985 projections, a developed-world growth rate 1 per cent lower in each year would cut the growth of the non-oil developing countries by one percentage point. Some 0.3 per cent of this cut would be due to the direct effects of the slow-down in export growth and some 0.7 per cent to the additional constraint imposed on imports if no extra finance were made available.[3] One point off industrial-country growth, as projected by the IMF, would postpone the recovery of 1980 levels of GDP per head in Latin America until the mid-1990s. The pressures for default would clearly be acute.

An improvement in the industrial countries' growth prospect

to just over 4 per cent a year, unlikely as that may seem, would equally add about one percentage point to non-oil developing-country growth even if there were no change in financing. The extension of 'new money' which the IMF assumes would also be more plausible if the industrial countries did indeed grow this quickly. But if there were no increase in 'new money' over projected levels, the need for debtor trade surpluses and negative transfers would remain the same, even if they were to account for a smaller share of total exports and would in addition be easier to bear because of healthier debtor growth. Moreover, higher industrial-country growth would not benefit all countries equally, despite the assumption in some of the most influential debt-projection studies that it would.[4] As the IMF itself has pointed out, the recovery in the industrial countries has been of disproportionate benefit to the Asian countries and less so to some of the other major debtors.[5] Even a substantially better industrial-country growth performance than that projected by the Fund would provide no guarantee that the debt crisis would be resolved.

Another objection to the IMF baseline scenario and other projections is that no explicit allowance is made for the influence of the trade cycle: the industrial world is projected to grow at a fairly steady pace, with no new recession over the forecast period. Any dip in growth, even if it were subsequently made up so that the average rate remained the same, might seriously prejudice the debtor countries' positions. Nor is it much consolation that developed-world growth in 1984 was rather better than the previous projections had forecast. That has certainly reduced the levels of the fashionable creditworthiness ratios, but it has had no demonstrable effect on the banks' willingness to lend and has been extraordinarily dependent on an American trade deficit which must eventually dwindle. It is likely to be of little consolation to a debtor country which finds itself in a new recession with a large negative transfer and foreign exchange running short. The world of rosy debt projections is a world without the strains of trade cycles. Economic history does not encourage optimism on this score.

For all of these reasons we are distrustful of the conventional wisdom that about 3 per cent industrial-country growth each year represents some sort of 'critical threshold' which is a necessary (if not a sufficient) condition for resolving the debt crisis; the figure has been given credence by the IMF, William Cline's influential study[6] and the forecasts of Morgan Guaranty, one of the leading bank analysts of the debt problem.[7] The sophistication of the mathematics which goes into these projections is not accompanied by any unanimity of view about certain key numbers. Though each of these forecasters has argued that around 3 per cent annual growth is crucial, the debtor-country current-account deficits which each study throws up are very different. This suggests that each of them has a rather different view of what might constitute manageability. Cline himself compares his work with the IMF's 1983 projections and finds that the current-account deficit of the non-oil developing countries forecast at that time for 1986 was likely to be $52.5 billion compared with $93 billion in the IMF research.[8] Probably the best that we can say with confidence is that the world would be a lot easier to live in if industrial-country growth were relatively high, but that high growth is not in itself a way out of the debt problem.[9]

A further reason for caution in selecting 'magic numbers' for this or that economic factor is the extent of the uncertainty which surrounds the link between import growth and the growth of the economy as a whole in debtor countries. The extraordinary cuts in import volumes in Latin America of 19 per cent in 1982 and 27 per cent in 1983,[10] the principal cause of the conversion of the trade deficits into surpluses, are unsustainable, as even the IMF managing director has admitted.[11] Indeed, in 1984 Latin America's imports rose by 4.7 per cent, with an estimated growth of GDP of only 2.6 per cent. Some of the debtors may in future be able to rely on lower import growth relative to the growth of their national income than has been the case historically. For example, part of Brazil's import decline has been due to long-standing projects for import substitution, such as the powering of cars by gasohol rather than oil. But a reversion to anything near the historical relationship between imports and growth is likely to mean the need either for more foreign exchange or for lower growth rates than are likely to be compatible with political stability.

The difficulty of pinning down the link between imports and growth can be seen in Figure 3, which shows a very steep rise in import volumes (excluding the more predictable elements of oil and wheat) compared with real GDP over the period to 1974.

This was followed by a decline to 1978, a period when import volume merely kept pace with GDP, and then a steep fall (by nearly 50 per cent) from 1980 to 1983. The extent to which feasible import growth translates into feasible GDP growth depends on a future view of the link; studies show anything from a mere 0.8 per cent import growth for 1 per cent GDP growth to 2 per cent import growth for 1 per cent GDP growth. The 7.2 per cent annual growth of import volume for the rest of the decade which the IMF assumes for its western hemisphere

Figure 3   Brazil: real GDP and non-oil import volume 1963–83
(Indices: 1977 = 100)

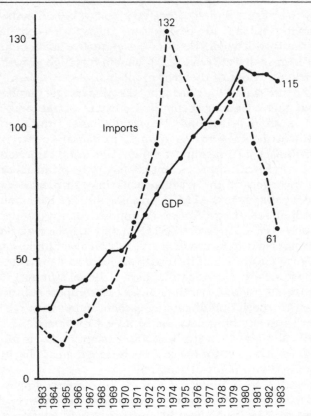

Source: Rudiger Dornbusch, 'The Debt Problem: 1980–84 and Beyond' (mimeo), MIT, Boston, 1985.

group could thus be consistent with growth rates varying from 3.5 per cent to 9 per cent a year. The IMF's forecasts are, in fact, cautious on this score, but some of the independent projections assume GDP/import relationships which allow surprisingly high growth for a given rise in imports.[12]

A further feature of most of the debt-projection studies is that interest rates will fall, thus gradually reducing the interest payment element of the negative transfer and improving debtor growth. The IMF base case, for example, assumes that real interest rates – after allowing for inflation – will fall by 3 per cent by 1990. Specifically, LIBOR for three-month dollar deposits – the key rate which, when the spread or bank profit is added, determines most commercial lending to the developing countries – will gradually decline from an average level of 10.8 per cent in 1984 to 8 per cent in 1990. (A rise in US inflation will account for the remainder of the real cut.)

This also seems eminently plausible. Indeed, at the time of writing three-month dollar LIBOR had already fallen to just over 8 per cent. Nevertheless, there is no swift salvation in lower interest rates. As we have seen, negative transfers, on the IMF's projections, remain very large despite the assumption of falling rates. In addition, the influence of interest rates on the average debtor's available foreign exchange, and hence growth, is limited. One percentage point more on LIBOR would cost the non-oil exporters some 0.7 per cent of their exports of goods and services, whereas 1 per cent less growth in the industrial world would amount to a loss of 3.3 per cent, on the Fund's calculations. In other words, a change of 1 per cent in growth is more than four times as powerful an influence on debtors' foreign exchange than a change of 1 per cent in the interest rates on which their borrowing costs depend. Clearly, the higher the debt, the more important are interest rates relative to industrial world growth. But even for the biggest debtors – Mexico and Brazil – Morgan Guaranty's calculations suggest that a 1 per cent change in LIBOR and a 1 per cent change in OECD area growth have about equal impact.[13]

A fall in the dollar, the currency in which developing-country debt is overwhelmingly denominated, might also be expected to have beneficial effects on the debt problem. Once again, however, the three most recent projections from the IMF, Morgan Guaranty and William Cline already build into their forecasts some decline in the American currency. (In the IMF's case, the dollar is projected to drop in real terms – after allowing for any difference between its inflation rate and that of its competitors – by nearly 1 per cent in 1986 and by just over 4 per cent a year from 1987 to 1990.)

A declining dollar has several effects on the debtors. It makes it more difficult for them to compete in the American market and with American goods in other markets. On the other hand, other foreign currency receipts are worth more dollars, and dollar imports are cheaper in domestic currency. Other imports rise in dollar value. The Cline and Morgan Guaranty studies show that the *net* effect of a weaker dollar is to increase the size of debtor current-account deficits when expressed in dollars and to increase dollar debt. Because it also raises the dollar value of exports, the effect is marginally to improve creditworthiness ratios such as the debt to export ratio.

In Morgan's work a 5 per cent drop in the dollar in each of 1985 and 1986 would cut the proportion of Brazil's exports theoretically earmarked for interest payments (before offsetting 'new money') from 33 per cent in 1986 to 32 per cent. In Mexico there would be no change at all. One reason why the effect of a dollar fall is so small is simply that so many of Latin America's exports are priced in the American currency, and it may take some time before prices respond to a fall in the value of the *numéraire* (the unit or the currency) in which they are expressed. The effect of a dollar fall on the major debtors could even be slightly unfavourable if the banks did not prove willing to increase 'new money' in dollars to offset the fall in its worth. In any event, changes in the dollar's parity are unlikely radically to affect the debt problem one way or another.

The same cannot be said of changes in oil prices; almost any sudden and sharp shift, either upwards or downwards, would be bound to send some debt skittles flying. The risks for the banks are probably rather greater if there is a large fall because some of the biggest debtors – notably Venezuela and Mexico – are particularly reliant on oil exports. Though oil-importing debtors like Brazil would clearly benefit, the effects would be more diffuse. Thus Morgan Guaranty calculates that a 10 per cent drop in oil prices would cut Brazil's current-account deficit in 1986 by $800 million but would add $2 billion to Mexico's. Overall, a sharp fall in oil prices should clearly be of benefit to world trade and to the developing countries, most of which are still oil importers. The secondary effect, however, could be to spark off a wave of defaults on debt in Mexico, Venezuela, Nigeria and other oil exporters. The oil shocks of the 1970s cannot safely be reversed without upsetting many of the structures which grew up in response to them.

Perhaps most contentious of all the assumptions of the debt-projection studies, including that of the IMF, is the notion that protectionism in the developed world will not tighten, and hence will not erode the hitherto strong links between industrial-country growth and export buoyancy in the Third World. The reality is that barriers to debtor-country exports continue to mount. This has a clear economic dimension, in that the industrial countries are in effect hampering the only means by which the debtors can service their debts. It also has a political one, for little that the industrial countries do appears more hypocritical or provocative to the debtors than an insistence on sacrifice to honour debts while protecting their own industries from change.

The irony is that such protectionism against the debtor countries largely redistributes unemployment within the developed world. Indeed, overall the effects are uniformly negative. Where debtor-country imports are tightly constrained by the lack of adequate finance, it follows that each cut in a debtor's exports is likely to be matched by a cut in industrial-country exports. What one set of producers may gain, others are likely to lose in equivalent amounts. For the potential purchaser who is unable to buy the foreign product, the loss of welfare is direct and clear. In these circumstances protectionism against the Third World involves losses all round.

Yet there can be no doubt about the recent trend. Successive rounds of multilateral negotiations through GATT have steadily reduced tariff duties on industrial products from about 40 per cent in the mid-1930s to just below 7 per cent once the agreements in the Tokyo round come into effect,[14] but this process of liberalization has been offset by two factors. The first is the breakdown of the Bretton Woods system of relatively stable exchange rates and the institution instead of floating rates which can vary so quickly and to such an extent as to make perfectly efficient businesses uncompetitive within weeks. The second and more insidious factor, in part a consequence of misaligned exchange rates, is the rapid growth in non-tariff barriers to trade. These can take the form of overt quantitative restrictions limiting the imports of a particular good to a specific number of units. They can be 'voluntary' export restraints agreed by the exporting country for fear of something worse. Or often protectionism masquerades as bogus safety and technical standards.

Some of the developing countries with the heaviest debt burdens face the greatest hurdles in exporting. As the UNCTAD estimates in Table 7 show, 27.7 per cent of the EEC's imports from developing America are subject to non-tariff barriers compared with an average 17.3 per cent across the various groups of exporters cited. In the United States too South America is subject to slightly higher degrees of restraint than the average.

Table 7   Share of selected developed market-economy countries' imports subject to non-tariff barriers: total imports by major groups of exporters (%)

IMPORTERS/EXPORTERS	UNITED STATES	JAPAN	EEC	SWITZER- LAND	SWEDEN	NORWAY	AUSTRIA
Developing America	7.3	18.5	27.7	36.3	32.2	21.7	37.7
Developing Africa	0.8	10.6	10.4	85.2	2.7	14.0	2.8
Developing Asia and Pacific	10.2	4.8	9.9	53.2	8.4	11.6	3.0
Socialist countries of Eastern Europe	10.4	16.4	34.1	75.9	3.7	40.0	4.2
Socialist countries of Asia	40.1	11.8	32.7	17.2	8.3	10.3	5.8
Developed market-economy countries	6.8	19.9	19.7	22.7	4.5	10.1	6.7
Total	6.9	11.4	17.3	27.4	5.9	11.0	6.7

Source: UNCTAD, *Trade and Development Report 1984 (TDR/4*, Vol. II), Part 2, 17 July 1984.

Primary commodities still account for about four-fifths of Latin America's exports. Their treatment by the developing world varies according to whether they are farm or non-farm goods. Agricultural products have traditionally been subject to heavy degrees of protection, but the growth of the market is anyway limited because consumption does not tend to rise as fast as aggregate incomes. This creates its own problems when the developed economies have farm sectors whose revenues they are attempting to keep broadly in line with national growth. As a result of high support prices, the most heavily protectionist part of the world in farm products, the EEC, has chronic food surpluses which it then dumps on world markets to the detriment of the prices which more efficient producers can obtain. Nor is the USA blameless. In 1982 the quota on sugar imports from Brazil into the USA was reduced from 1 million tons to 400,000 tons at a cost at then ruling prices of $150 million annually.[15] Inevitably such restrictions raise the price in the protected area and lower it outside. In July 1984 the world free-market sugar price was 4.5 US cents per pound, and in the USA it was 22 cents.[16]

There is little or no protection against non-agricultural primary commodities because of their use as raw materials and the rarity of powerful domestic producer groups in the developed countries. But equally demand for primary commodities does not expand as quickly as manufactures in part because of technological change. For example, the advent of micro-circuitry has reduced the need for Chile's main commodity – copper for electrical connections. In addition, the development of near-substitutes for many traditional materials also cuts potential Third World exports. For example, Bolivia has been hit by the use of plastics rather than tin in packaging.

It is precisely in relatively fast-growing trade in semi-finished and finished manufactures that developed-country protectionism has hit hardest. The GATT Secretariat has estimated that the proportion of total OECD-area trade covered by non-tariff barriers had risen from 36 per cent in 1974 to 44 per cent in 1980, but within that total the coverage of manufactures had risen from 4 per cent to 20 per cent.[17] In other words, the impact of industrial-country protectionism is all the greater because it affects those areas where the debtor exporters might expect to make most gains. Either protectionism hits them where the market is growing most quickly, or its impact is in areas of traditional and largely labour-intensive manufactures like textiles, where the debtor exporters could make gains because of their comparative advantage in lower labour costs.

One of the most notorious examples is the Multi-Fibre Arrangement (MFA), under which imports of textiles and clothing into the developed world are strictly limited by bilateral quotas for specific product groups. The gradual tightening of the MFA during its various renegotiations in the 1970s and early 1980s has provided some windfall gains for Third World producers who have been able to sell limited quantities at higher prices because of the lack of competition, but the overall effect has been both to freeze relatively inefficient producers into their historical market shares and to remove a rung of the export ladder by which newly industrializing countries were able to upgrade the value added of their exports. For example, Mexican textile exports to the USA actually fell from $114 million in 1979 to $96 million in 1983 – a decline, as a proportion of Mexican exports, from 1.9 per cent to 0.8 per cent.[18] In December 1983 the Reagan administration further tightened textile protection with a new system of 'consultations' whenever the share of imports in total consumption of the product exceeded trigger levels.[19]

High unemployment in Europe and the over-valuation of the dollar have combined to increase the willingness of the advanced countries to resort to so-called anti-dumping and countervailing duty procedures. The number of these measures increased from 124 in 1979 to 405 in 1982, while the proportion which was aimed at developing countries' producers rose from 17 per cent to 26 per cent.[20] There are ominous signs that such cases could be extended to areas where some of the big debtors have managed to gain market shares. For example, the 1984 election year in the USA saw producers of steel, copper and footwear file for new protection under the safeguard mechanisms of US law. The US International Trade Commission had ruled that injury to domestic producers – a necessary condition – was established for both steel (of interest particularly to Brazil and Mexico) and copper (of interest to Chile).[21] In Mexico's case the administration imposed countervailing duties on such exports as steel, car parts, ceramic tiles, leather garments and construction materials during 1983 and 1984, without even the formality of establishing domestic injury, on the grounds that Mexico is not a member of GATT or a signatory to its subsidy code.[22]

It is all too easy to recite long lists of developing-country exports which have been hindered by protection; by definition, it is harder to quantify the damage to their exports and interests. But there is one worrying sign that developed-world protectionism is beginning to have much more impact than had hitherto been supposed. As the IMF has pointed out, one would expect the array of Fund-inspired policy measures designed to improve the developing countries' share of world markets, such as devaluations and the relatively depressed state of their domestic economies, would have begun to have some effect. Surprisingly, though, the increase in non-oil developing countries' exports to the OECD area since 1982 has been attributable entirely to the growth of the industrial countries' markets and does not seem to reflect gains in the developing countries' share of those markets[23] (see Figure 4). It is difficult to escape the conclusion that protectionism must be the main culprit.

There is very little chance that the momentum of protectionist sentiment in the developed world can be rolled back so long as

Figure 4   Non-oil developing countries: performance of exports to industrial countries 1978–84 (indices: 1980 = 100)

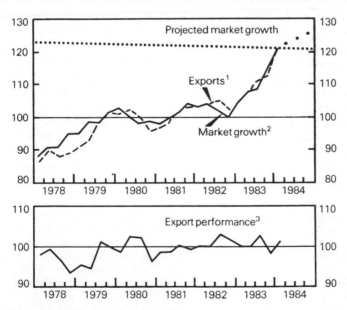

Notes: [1] Exports to industrial countries, as reported by the latter, deflated by export unit values of non-oil developing countries.
[2] Imports, in volume, of nineteen industrial countries weighted by their respective shares of non-oil developing countries' exports in 1980.
[3] Ratio of exports to market growth.

Source: IMF, *World Economic Outlook*, Washington DC, September 1984.

its chief fomenters during the last decade – stagflation and woeful exchange-rate misalignments – persist. The American administration's insistence in 1985 on an early start to a new GATT round was seen by its partners as essentially a defensive measure to stave off the mounting pile of protectionist Bills in Congress, and even that initiative fell foul of French resistance at the Bonn Western economic summit in May 1985. Even if a new round of GATT negotiations were launched early in 1986, it is hard to see it having any serious impact while the currency turmoil and stagflation persist.

One GATT round of negotiations, the Tokyo round, has already taken place in the last decade, but analysts universally find that protectionism has increased over the period. With the persistence of high levels of idle manpower and machinery, the political and social conditions for trade liberalization do not exist. Expansion must come first, as the founding fathers of the post-war economic order recognized. Until the situation changes, a new GATT round will permit only paper gains against a reality of mounting protectionism.

Indeed, there is a real risk that the closing off of trading opportunities to the Third World could prove to be the decisive factor which finally undermines the structure of the debt. It was, after all, by exactly this means that many of today's biggest debtor countries finally came to default in the 1930s. There is a striking and ominous presentiment in the following quotation. It could have been written today. In fact, it comes from the League of Nations' *World Economic Survey* of August 1932:

When the great creditor countries reduce their exports of capital, the very fact of reduction creates a situation in which all their debtors must meet their obligations either in goods or in gold, instead of by fresh borrowing. A strain is immediately placed upon the credit systems of the debtor countries. A deflation of prices is imposed upon them, the terms of trade become less advantageous, imports are restricted by lower purchasing power and exports are stimulated. If the financial situation becomes acute, these economic reactions may be supplemented by government intervention – for example, by restrictions on imports or by domestic retrenchment. The net effect of the curtailment of capital imports is therefore a strong pressure to provide an active export balance in commodity trade . . .

All of these phenomena were in evidence in many debtor countries in 1929, but the collapse of the American Stock Exchange boom in October of that year made credit conditions easier, particularly in the London money market, for a few months in early 1930. As prices continued to fall, however, the risks of lending became greater. New issues of foreign loans in the chief capital markets fell to such low levels that there was on balance a considerable net export of capital from debtor to creditor countries in 1931. The United Kingdom, for example, had a very substantial net inflow of capital in 1931, while France increased her net imports very substantially and the net exports from the United States of America were probably very small.

Before this extraordinary situation had fully developed, however, a further check was imposed upon the capacity of the debtor countries to pay their external obligations. The increased export surpluses which they placed upon world markets caused concern in the importing creditor countries, which thereupon imposed higher tariffs and supplemented them by additional restrictions on imports ... By the beginning of 1932, the creditor countries had become unanimous in refusing to receive payment from their debtors in the only form by which it was possible for the debtors to pay.

There ensued in consequence an enormous shrinkage in world trade, and the logical consequence of this shrinkage has been a series of moratoria, suspensions of payment, and standstill agreements, as a result of which the credit of many debtor countries has been gravely impaired ...

As early as January 1932, ominous defaults occurred upon what were even a few months before regarded as sound external loans ... National and individual bankruptcies and repudiations of debt on a vaster scale than the world has ever seen are imminent unless international trade can once more be restored to something approaching its former freedom.[24]

The following year's report (1933) notes that in the period under consideration loans of Ecuador, Mexico, Turkey, Bolivia, Peru, Chile, Brazil, Uruguay, Argentina, Dominica, Colombia, Nicaragua, Salvador and China were in default.

Happily, neither world trade or prices are now falling. But protectionism in the developed world today is only one of the threats to the world's financial system. The economic projections which insist that the debts will be serviced are riddled with unreal assumptions. It might be possible to envisage some success for the IMF's approach to the debt crisis if at least some of the conditions which need to be met could be dropped. The problem is that almost all of them need to be met. The industrial world has to grow relatively quickly. It has to keep its export markets open. Oil prices must not move sharply either up or down. Moreover, any slight divergence in one of these factors could only too easily be compounded by changes in the others. Tight monetary policy and high interest rates could cause a slow-down in growth, a fall in oil prices and mounting protection. Even if the advanced countries can walk this tight-rope, we saw in the preceding chapter that two further and vital conditions must be met. The advanced countries' banks have to be prepared to increase their exposures to the developing countries despite the experience of 1982, and the developing countries themselves have to resist the temptation to use the trade surpluses earmarked for debt-service dollars to increase their imports, growth and living standards instead. Every number on the IMF's card has to come up, and then the prize is merely to get us back to where the crisis began.

7

THE POLITICAL ECONOMY OF DEFAULT

Economic forces are in fact political forces.
The science of economics presupposes a given
political order, and cannot be profitably studied
in isolation from politics.

E. H. CARR

The characteristic danger of great nations
is that they may at last fail from
not comprehending the great institutions which
they have created.

WALTER BAGEHOT

Every debtor country which has had to reschedule its debt since the crisis of 1982 has already defaulted on the terms of its original obligations, though the formal acknowledgement of that default has so far been largely postponed. In this chapter we argue that such a papering over of the deep fissures in the financial system cannot be expected to persist. We look at the circumstances, pressures and temptations in some of the major debtor countries which could make even the pretence of a co-operative solution between creditors and debtors wholly untenable. Though in our view it will not be in the interest of any major debtor to repudiate its obligations outright, a steady and often unilateral erosion of the large negative transfers expected by the I M F and the banks will inevitably produce a widespread perception of default. That in turn can be expected to produce similar injury to the vital functioning of the advanced countries' largest banks.

We look particularly at the three Latin American debtor countries – Brazil, Mexico and Argentina – which between them account for more than one-quarter of all Third World debt (including official debt) and some 40 per cent of all Third World debt to the private banks.[1] These countries are so central to the debt crisis that the issue of whether current policies are sustainable cannot be resolved favourably unless it is resolved here. This is not to argue that other debtors are unimportant for individual large banks or are not equally or more hard-pressed by the conflicting requirements of debt service and domestic growth. For example, in the summer of 1985 Mr Alan Garcia, the new President of Peru, announced a unilateral limit on debt service worth 10 per cent of his country's exports, roughly half of what had been required under the previous rescheduling agreement or, indeed, paid out in 1984. Moreover, Mr Garcia said that he would not sign any new economic programme with the IMF. Henceforth Peru's debt would undergo 'automatic rescheduling'.[2] Nevertheless, Peru's bank debt of about $7.4 billion[3] does not in itself pose a threat to the entire banking system, though the example of the Peruvian government most certainly does. Mr Garcia's progress was being watched closely both by bigger debtors and by their apprehensive bankers. If his attempt to impose limits on negative transfers were to spread to Latin America's biggest debtors, a banking crisis could not long be averted. The political and economic importance of Mexico, Brazil and Argentina makes failure in these countries unthinkable and justifies our focus here on their prospects. Yet failure, unless policies are changed, looks only too probable.

There can be no serious presumption that the political and social systems of Latin America afford its policy-makers the luxury of taking a long view of the debt issue. All the main debtor countries are characterized by a series of potentially combustible elements. The overall level of income per person is low and has fallen in real terms since the end of the 1970s. That income is in turn maldistributed, so that the gulf between the rich and the poor is large and conspicuous. In the modern part of their economies the new working class, which was funnelled from the villages to work in the factories in the 1960s and 1970s, is increasingly militant in defence of its living standards and its right to work. The urban middle class, which has had rising expectations fostered by a decade of prospering businesses, cosmopolitan imports and foreign travel, now finds the prospect of consolidating its gains receding rapidly. In the rural areas land ownership remains concentrated in a tiny number of hands, and the landless suffer absolute poverty and malnutrition.

On the measures used by the World Bank, most of the big Latin American debtors have an average income per head which places them among the globe's 'upper-middle-income' countries. They are not among the poorest of the poor: Brazil's real income per head, for example, is some four times the Indian equivalent. But neither can they be described as wealthy. On the World Bank's estimates, income per head ranges from 17 to 19 per cent of the American level. However, this comparison does not take account of the relative cheapness of non-traded goods and services in countries which have low cash incomes and labour costs. On the more sophisticated measure of purchasing-power parity, which makes adjustments for these differences, the level of income per head in Mexico and Brazil is between 26 per cent and 31 per cent of the American level, as Table 8 shows. (Data on this basis are not available for other Latin American countries, though the pattern will tend to be similar to that of the World Bank figures, with Venezuela at the top of the Latin American scale and the poor Andean countries like Peru and Ecuador at the bottom.) They are thus 'upper-middle-income' only in the sense that they stand between the poorest developing countries and the First World: Mexican and Brazilian incomes per head are less than half the levels of the developed countries.

Table 8   GNP per head

	GNP PER HEAD, 1982 ($)	AS PERCENTAGE OF US GNP PER HEAD, 1982	REAL GNP PER HEAD, 1977 ($)	AS PERCENTAGE OF US GNP PER HEAD, PPP 1977
Mexico	2,270	17.3	2,413	31.1
Argentina	2,520	19.1		
Brazil	2,240	17.0	1,993	25.7
Venezuela	4,140	31.5		
Chile	2,210	16.8		
Peru	1,310	10.0		
Colombia	1,460	11.1		
USA	13,160	100.0	7,751	100.0
UK	9,660	73.4	4,863	62.4

Sources: GNP per head in 1982 from World Bank, *World Development Report*, Washington DC, 1984, pp. 218, 219; GNP per head at purchasing power parity (PPP) from Irving B. Kravis, Alan Heston and Robert Summers, *World Product and Income: International Comparisons of Real Gross Product*, Johns Hopkins University Press, Baltimore, 1982, Table 8.4, p. 336 (1975 prices).

This relatively low level of income is exceptionally unequal in its distribution. The most egalitarian of the Latin American countries for which figures are readily available is Argentina, and yet its distribution of income is still marginally *more* unequal than that of the United States, itself the most unequal of all the industrial market economies. The most glaring inequality, as Table 9 shows, occurs in Brazil where, at the time of the last survey, the bottom fifth of the population shared just 2 per cent of household income, while the top 10 per cent took 51 per cent. Moreover, this pattern appears to most observers to have grown worse in recent years, as the burden of depression has fallen most sharply on the poor. As the Final Document of the Catholic Conference of Latin American Bishops at Puebla, Mexico, recognized in 1979, there was a 'growing gap between rich and poor', which it characterized as a 'contradiction of Christian existence'.[4] In the twelve months up to October 1982 the number of Brazilians earning *less than half* of the official minimum wage of $73 a month increased by one-third to more than 10 million. According to census data, 41 per cent of the economically active population in late 1982 earned less than the minimum wage (defined as the level necessary to support a family of four) compared with 32 per cent a year earlier.[5]

Table 9   Income distribution: share of household income, in quintiles, of all households ranked by income

	LOWEST FIFTH (%)	SECOND FIFTH (%)	THIRD FIFTH (%)	FOURTH FIFTH (%)	TOP FIFTH (%)	TOP TENTH (%)
Brazil (1971)	2.0	5.0	9.4	17.0	66.6	50.6
Mexico (1977)	2.9	7.0	12.0	20.4	57.7	40.6
Argentina (1970)	4.4	9.7	14.1	21.5	50.3	35.2
Venezuela (1970)	3.0	7.3	12.9	22.8	54.0	35.7
Peru (1972)	1.9	5.1	11.0	21.0	61.0	42.9
USA (1978)	4.6	8.9	14.1	22.1	50.3	33.4
UK (1979)	7.0	11.5	17.0	24.8	39.7	23.4
Japan (1979)	8.7	13.2	17.5	23.1	36.8	21.2

Source: World Bank, *World Development Report*, Washington D C, 1984, Table 28, pp. 272–3. Dates of surveys are in brackets after each country's name.

A further consequence of the recession has been the large-scale shedding of jobs. In Brazil the number of jobs had fallen in 1983 to the level of a decade before despite population growth estimated at 25 million.[6] The poor who had flocked from the rural areas during the high-growth years of the 1960s and 1970s, escaping a concentration of land tenure which in the north-east of Brazil puts 45 per cent of the acreage in the hands of 1 per cent of the landowners, began to find that the shanty towns which had grown up outside Latin America's cities were another instance of the same trap.[7] In São Paulo, Brazil's largest city, 400,000 jobs were lost in just three years.[8]

The social consequences have been dramatic. Malnutrition has spread to more than one-third of the populations of Mexico and Brazil, according to reports of the World Health Organization and government estimates.[9] Scavengers root among the garbage tips of São Paulo waiting for the arrival of each new truck. Sporadic riots and looting have occurred on a scale not seen for decades. Between September 1983 and March 1984, 225 supermarkets, warehouses and shops were reported to have been looted in São Paulo, Rio de Janeiro and the north-east of Brazil.[10] Those involved appear to have been the poorest of the poor, who had nothing left to lose. In the northern regions of Mexico, close to the American border, the unrest has taken on a more political character, with suspicions that it is in support of, if not supported by, the right-wing opposition party, the National Action Party (PAN). In one incident a local police chief was crucified and then stoned to death by the mob.[11]

The Mexican government has so far succeeded in containing labour unrest through the links of the ruling Institutional Revolutionary Party (PRI) with organized labour. The new governments of Brazil and Argentina have been less fortunate. The sharply rising inflation rates which were the legacy of the twin impact of devaluations and a wages scramble for shares of a shrinking cake have in turn added new twists to labour militancy. Within six months of taking office in December 1983 Argentina's President, Raul Alfonsín, was facing the threat of a 'battle plan' of protests and strikes from the Confederacion General del Trabajo (CGT), the main union movement associated with the Perónist opposition. The government had promised real wage rises of between 6 and 8 per cent in its first year. Throughout June 1984 it was besieged by strikes involving an estimated 2 million workers who were pressing for increases amounting to treble the government's guidelines. Inflation accelerated to a rate of 675 per cent in 1984. Real wages lagged behind, and Alfonsín appeared to be in increasing trouble over his attempts to secure a *concertacion* with the CGT. In the first half of 1985 inflation sped up to more than 1,000 per cent a year. The most popular slogan of the widespread union protests in May was 'No to the IMF'.

In Brazil the closing months of the military regime of General Figueiredo were marked by a wave of social unrest, which included some bitter industrial disputes. In May 1984 pickets armed with knives were reported to be menacing São Paulo bus drivers to strike in pursuit of wage increases. At the same time sugar-cane cutters and orange pickers were also involved in a dispute which caused clashes with the police, several injuries and a death. A year later the new government of President José Sarney, who took over after the death of Tancredo Neves, faced a prolonged stoppage in São Paulo which embroiled 120,000 workers, including the important motor industry. Inflation accelerated gently from a rate of 179 per cent in 1983 to 194 per cent in 1984.

A moratorium on debt is no longer an unmentionable political issue. It has been the stock in trade of left-wing opposition figures for some time. In Argentina the socialist and human rights campaigner Luís Zamora, like the CGT and much of the Perónist leadership, has backed a break with the IMF and has added with brutal clarity that if creditors sought to freeze Argentinian assets abroad, the response could be to expropriate foreign holdings in Argentina: 'They've got much more to lose than us.'[12] In Brazil Luís Ignacio da Silva (or 'Lula'), the São Paulo trade union and Workers' Party leader, points out that the workers are not the people who borrowed the money, yet they are expected to repay it with cuts in living standards. In October 1983 the Brazilian opposition leader, Mr Ulysses Guimaraes, said that accepting IMF terms was tantamount to an abdication of national sovereignty, and his Brazilian Democratic Movement backed a moratorium.

These notions, moreover, extended well into the technocracy and more establishment parts of the political spectrum. Mr Anibal Pinto, a leading Latin American economist, called the IMF's terms for Brazil 'manifestly absurd' and put his weight behind a moratorium.[13] In reaction to the Western economic summit in Bonn in 1985, four Argentinian senators of the President's own right-of-centre Radical Party called on the government to insist on a 'more flexible' approach from creditors and a limit to the proportion of exports which should go in debt payments. The example of Mr Garcia's 10 per cent limit in Peru, which parallels ideas current in Argentina, was also reported to be under consideration by President José Sarney of Brazil.[14] The combination of severe, if sporadic, social disorder and the political pressure of the middle class for rising living standards is a potent force for change.

Until now Latin American leaders – especially those of the key debtor countries – have been careful to avoid radical, and particularly collective, action. The attempts to put together some sort of 'debtors' cartel' through the Cartagena group have been in reality more of a debtors' lobby. There have certainly been joint policy pronouncements, expressions of concern over high dollar interest rates and, most recently, a statement issued (shortly after Mr Garcia's announcement) which endorses the general principle of linking debt service to ability to pay. But the cartel has not been formed, in part because some of its key participants clearly believe that they may be able to secure better treatment by bargaining individually rather than by aligning themselves with some of the more notorious bad debtors among the smaller countries.

There has also been the fear that joint action would appear needlessly provocative when there are still high hopes that advanced-country governments will be able to meet some of the debtors' concerns. Most of Latin America's leaders have no desire to align themselves with the strident calls for repudiation from Cuba's President Fidel Castro, who is perceived as attempting to make as much self-serving mischief as he can.

These considerations may well rule out the bankers' nightmare of a joint Latin American default on debt, but they do not rule out a steady process of conciliatory, even apologetic, but nevertheless unilateral limits on debt service. Unless the hope is kept alive that there can be a decisive policy change in the advanced countries that will lift the burden of debt, the learning curve of the debtors' governments, combined with the political and economic pressures of their people, will lead them inevitably to take matters into their own hands.

A look, country by country, at the amounts of foreign exchange which these major debtors are expected to transfer to their creditors over the next few years is enough to underline the truly Herculean task which the IMF has set them. As we have seen, the IMF does not make publicly available its forecasts of individual members. In Chapter 5 we had to look at aggregated groups of debtors to form some idea of what the I M F projects. Here, in order to give an order of magnitude for each of the three key Latin American debtors, we take instead three reputable forecasts of the debt position of these countries (see Tables 10, 11 and 12) and derive from them the implied net transfer of foreign exchange from each over the period to 1989.[15]

All of these independent forecasts show that each of these countries has to make very substantial net payments, though inevitably the exact size of the projected transfers differs (reflecting primarily different assumptions about bank lending and interest rates). In the case of Argentina in 1987 (see Table 10), the net transfer to creditors is expected to be a minimum of $3.7 billion, in the forecast of Wharton Econometric Forecasting Associates, and a maximum of $4.99 billion, in the forecast of Data Resources, Inc. (DRI). Professor William Cline of the Institute for International Economics in Washington takes a middle view, at $4.2 billion. These figures represent a range of between 26 per cent and 35 per cent of total exports of goods

Table 10   Argentina's projected net transfers 1985–9: three forecasts ($ million)

	1985	1987	1989
CLINE			
Interest	− $6,205	− $5,549	n.a.
Net new borrowing	+ $3,424	+ $1,398	n.a.
Net transfer	− $2,781	− $4,151	
DRI			
Interest	− $5,790	− $6,640	− $6,121
Net new borrowing	+ $1,979	+ $1,649	+ $263
Net transfer	− $3,811	− $4,991	− $5,858
WHARTON			
Interest	− $7,300	− $5,700	− $7,400
Net new borrowing	+ $900	+ $2,000	+ $200
Net transfer	− $6,400	− $3,700	− $7,200

Sources: William R. Cline, *International Debt: Systemic Risk and Policy Response*, Institute for International Economics, Washington D C, 1984, p. 165; Data Resources, Inc., *Latin American Review*, Winter 1984; Wharton Econometric Forecasting Associates, *Latin American Economic Outlook*, October 1984; and authors' calculations.

Table 11   Brazil's projected net transfers 1985–9: three forecasts ($ million)

	1985	1987	1989
CLINE			
Interest	−$12,999	−$11,471	n.a.
Net new borrowing	+$4,478	+$312	n.a.
Net transfer	−$8,521	−$11,159	n.a.
DRI			
Interest	−$11,137	−$13,192	−$13,301
Net new borrowing	+$2,385	+$5,039	+$5,373
Net transfer	−$8,752	−$8,153	−$7,928
WHARTON			
Interest	−$15,100	−$10,700	−$14,000
Net new borrowing	−$2,000	+$3,200	—
Net transfer	−$17,100	−$7,500	−$14,000

Sources: As Table 10.

Table 12   Mexico's projected net transfers 1985–9: three forecasts ($ million)

	1985	1987	1989
CLINE			
Interest	−$10,693	−$8,852	n.a.
Net new borrowing	+$1,642	−$1,728	n.a.
Net transfer	−$9,051	−$10,580	
DRI			
Interest	−$11,740	−$13,219	−$13,323
Net new borrowing	+$2,729	+$5,627	+$5,311
Net transfer	−$9,011	−$7,592	−$8,012
WHARTON			
Interest	−$13,500	−$9,900	−$13,200
Net new borrowing	+$1,300	+$2,500	+$5,300
Net transfer	−$12,200	−$7,400	−$7,900

Sources: As Table 10.

and services. Moreover, they continue throughout the period on all the forecasts (i.e. until 1987 in the case of Cline, until 1989 in those of DRI and Wharton). It seems that no one has the temerity to suppose that the confidence of the international banking system in Argentina's prospects will revive sufficiently to ensure positive transfers once again.

Argentina is not exceptional. As Tables 11 and 12 show, the forecasts for Brazil and Mexico also indicate negative transfers which are larger in money terms (reflecting their bigger economies). Moreover, the two independent forecasters (D R I and Wharton), which make longer-term projections, foresee that the net transfer in cash terms either is roughly stable or actually rises until 1989. (D R I forecasts a very small cash fall in the net transfer between 1987 and 1989.) In Brazil's case the forecasts show negative transfers ranging from 22 per cent to 28 per cent of total exports in 1987. In Mexico's case the proportions range from 18 per cent of exports to 35 per cent. Further into the future the prospect is not much better. The D R I and Wharton forecasts project the perverse transfer in 1989 at 16 per cent from Mexico and between 20 per cent and 35 per cent from Brazil.

These projected figures represent such an enormous adverse flow of resources that we find it simply incredible to assume that the debtors' governments will be able and willing to make the sacrifices required, even given a favourable world environment. After all, the negative transfers also represent very real forgone opportunities for higher imports, growth and living standards. This conclusion, indeed, has worried some analysts and policy-makers so much that they have sought to show either that there are long-term advantages in servicing debt which will outweigh these evident costs or, alternatively, that the costs of default would themselves be so severe as to act as a powerful deterrent. In our view, neither line of argument is convincing, and both fail lamentably to take account of the political, social and economic pressures which we have already outlined. Let us deal with each point in turn.

One clear long-term advantage of continued debt service is that commercial bank lending in theory allows a developing country to even out an income flow which might otherwise be buffeted by shocks, such as commodity price falls.[16] In practice, however, we have seen that the boom-and-bust cycle of over- and under-lending is likely to aggravate any cycles which the developing countries have to endure rather than to smooth them out. In theory, bank lending should have expanded markedly to offset the fall in commodity prices in 1981 and 1982. In fact, it dried up all but completely.

In any case, the prospect of a resumption of new lending on a scale adequate to staunch the negative transfers is a forlorn hope for anything but the far-distant future unless the banks are supported in the task by their governments. After all, the debtors turned to the banks to borrow the funds they needed in the 1970s precisely because the bond markets were no longer willing to provide money on such a scale. There were still too many memories of written-down and defaulted bonds in the 1930s. It is hardly likely that the banks, once burned by the crisis of 1982, will prove any more willing than private bond-holders to forget an unhappy past.

Of all the debtor countries which had to undergo a re-scheduling of their debts in the late 1970s and early 1980s, only one country has so far emerged in a state which the IMF might regard as normal, in the sense that positive transfers have once again resumed. Turkey, which had to reschedule its debt in 1978–9, suffered a net outflow of resources to the banks of $3 billion over the next five years, until it was able, in the second half of 1983, to secure a small net inflow of $297 million which continued at the same level in 1984.[17] However, Turkey is also quite unlike the major debtors in that official lending by Western governments and multilateral organizations accounts for $14 billion out of its total $19 billion of outstanding debt,[18] mainly because of its strategic importance in the south-eastern flank of NATO and its close links with West Germany. Bank exposures are consequently tiny by comparison with those of the major debtors. Mexico, with $72 billion of bank debt, and Brazil, with $77 billion, can scarcely draw comfort from the example.[19]

It thus seems clear that the major debtors can expect few advantages from their theoretical access to the international capital markets. This is perhaps why, every so often, some Western politician or monetary official warns about the consequences for the debtors' trade and well-being if they should even con-sider a default: the consequences of abiding by debt-service commitments may appear onerous, but the consequences of defaulting would be even worse. An example was Mr R. T. McNamar, Deputy Secretary of the US Treasury, speaking to the US Chamber of Commerce in 1983:

A second obligation of the [developing-country] debtors is to work with their creditors within the international financial system to bring about orderly rescheduling of their debt-service burdens ... A repudiation takes place when a borrower unilaterally renounces responsibility for some or all of his debt obligations. Under such circumstances, the foreign assets of a country would be attached by creditors throughout the world; its exports would be seized by creditors at each dock where they landed, its national airlines unable to operate, and its sources of desperately needed capital goods and spare parts virtually eliminated. In many countries, even food imports would be curtailed. Hardly a pleasant scenario.[20]

The reality, though, is very different. Most debtor assets held abroad belong not to the state which is likely to default but to individual citizens or private corporations: no creditor would succeed in getting a British or American court to attach these assets in lieu of payment on a *state* debt. There would be enormous difficulty in attaching even assets which belonged to legally separate entities owned by the state, such as airlines or other nationalized industries. Moreover, the most crucial category of state assets from the point of view of the defaulter, its foreign-exchange reserves, would almost certainly remain inviolable. In short, private creditors would be likely to face innumerable legal hurdles, with the only sure advantage of litigation accruing to the lawyers.[21]

Legislation in both the United States and Britain has attempted to limit a foreign borrower's immunity from suit by drawing a distinction between a state's commercial and state activities, and it has been used by many lawyers to insert waivers of state immunity into loan contracts. But the dividing line between what is commercial and what is a state act is far from clear. In one case in which an American bank sought redress against a defaulting foreign bank, the US Court of Appeals refused on the ground that it would mean insisting that the defaulting bank break the law of its own country, which would risk embarrassment to the US Government's foreign policy.[22]

Assuming that a private creditor managed to jump the hurdle of sovereign immunity, its next problem would be to enforce that judgment by attaching assets belonging to the debtor. Even under the new US Foreign Sovereign Immunities Act of 1976, enforcement is limited strictly to assets used specifically for commercial activities: this rules out immediately any notion of attaching embassy or consulate buildings or naval assets. Even here, there is a further difficulty: the debtor's commercial assets could easily be moved out of the range of the courts. As if all that were not enough, it is also likely that the defaulter's foreign exchange reserves would remain out of reach. True, official reserves held with a commercial bank could merely be offset against any loans owed to the bank. But most reserves are held with the Federal Reserve Bank of New York, and it would be reluctant to allow a private creditor to attach them, as an affidavit filed in 1984 by Anthony Solomon (then president) demonstrated. He pointed out that if foreign central banks feared that their assets might be seized, they could withdraw their dollar reserves, cause a significant liquidation of U S government securities, strain the ability of the U S Treasury to finance public debt, and destabilize the international monetary system.[23]

If a central bank decided not to risk the protection of the Federal Reserve Bank of New York, it would be at liberty to remove its holdings, even after a case against it had begun, to the absolute safety of the B I S in Basle or, indeed, to one of the anonymous or nominee accounts which the banks operate for customers in the off-shore banking centres.

In short, legal suits against sovereign governments are likely to prove lengthy, expensive and fruitless. A sovereign government's legal position in both English and American law, the systems under which most loan agreements are signed, is still distinct enough to make it quite different from a normal defaulting debtor at home. After a discussion of the various difficulties involved in pinning a sovereign state down in law, one authority recently concluded: 'Contractual and juridical devices cannot be a substitute for the good faith and credit of the borrower, which in the final analysis is the real protection on which lenders should rely in making loans to sovereign states.'[24]

The one lever which the banks have undoubtedly been able to apply to ensure debt service since 1982, despite the growing net outflows since that year, has been the threat of vanishing trade credit. As we saw in Chapter 2, this prospect could impose a very serious and abrupt negative transfer on the debtors by making them pay for imports on the nail while still having to await payments for exports. There would be no credit to bridge the gap: imports would have to shrink dramatically. A condition of default would thus be that the debtor is reasonably confident that it can weather this credit withdrawal through such measures as building up foreign-exchange reserves and increasing barter trade. As we have seen, both reserves and barter trade are rising.

However circumscribed may be the remedies of private creditors, it is nevertheless clear that in some circumstances legal harassment, including attachments, has proved remarkably costly to some countries. Two obvious examples were the seizure of Iranian assets during the hostage crisis in 1980 and the freeze on Argentinian assets in Britain following the outbreak of the Falklands/Malvinas conflict in 1982. The notable feature of both cases, though, was that private litigation played little or no part in them. They were acts of government, undertaken through executive order under emergency economic powers voted by the respective legislatures. They were not acts of the judiciary in Britain or the United States.[25]

But *state* sanctions cannot necessarily be triggered by *private* interests. Indeed, it is hard to see why today's Western governments would be any more anxious to retaliate against a defaulting Latin American state than they were in the 1930s, when the overwhelming argument against intervention that had been the response of earlier generations was that it might open the door to foreign influence. The United States in 1937 was concerned about the growing German presence in Brazil:[26] the State Department would hardly be less concerned today, even though the subject of that concern has shifted eastwards. The first priority of the advanced countries would be to defuse both the economic and the political crisis. It would be no part of Western intent to provide demagogic politicians with the ammunition to arouse populist clamour.

One attempt to quantify the costs and benefits of default, by Thomas Enders and Richard Mattione,[27] concludes that 'on economic grounds repudiation is not a better alternative' than debt service, though the study adds: 'The degree of danger involved in a prolonged crisis of debt and growth . . . is sufficiently great to justify every effort to manage the crisis through facilitating trade, adjusting exchange rates, promoting capital reforms and providing additional funds. The alternative could be unrest throughout the [Western] hemisphere.'

Their calculations tend, if anything, to underscore the risks involved. For each of the main Latin American debtors they show the difference, in national income (GDP) over five years, between a 'base case', in which the countries continue to service their debt, and two different scenarios for a default (assumed to have happened in 1982). In the case of a 5 per cent cost of repudiation they assume that the debtor has to pay 5 per cent more for its imports and, in addition, loses 5 per cent on the sale of its exports. In the second case they assume 10 per cent losses on both exports and imports. Nevertheless, in either default scenario Brazil, Argentina and Venezuela all have higher levels of national income at the end of the forecast period (1987) than they do in the study's base case. They also have higher levels of income, on average, throughout the 1983–7 projection. Mexico manages to reap net gains from a default if the trade costs do not exceed 5 per cent but loses out if the costs reach 10 per cent.

A cool look at some standard forecasts, along with some fairly optimistic assumptions about future bank lending, thus suggests that the danger of default cannot be dismissed lightly. The private calculations of the British government seem to come to the same conclusion, as a revealing parliamentary answer given by the Prime Minister, Mrs Thatcher, on 24 March 1983 implied. Mrs Thatcher was being pressed by the then leader of the Labour Party, Mr Michael Foot, about British participation in an IMF package of new finance for Argentina, which he feared might be spent on armaments (a sensitive issue in the light of the 1982 Falklands conflict). Mrs Thatcher said the government supported the package for two reasons:

First, in the absence of either the IMF or commercial loan there was a possibility that the Argentine would default. If she was to default she would have even more money to spend on arms than if she met the debt. That is a fact of life. Furthermore, unless she receives some help she could default to third countries and therefore trigger off collapse of difficult and delicate packages which have been reached through the IMF with those countries.

When pressed further for a reassurance that the money would not go on arms, Mrs Thatcher said that Mr Foot had still not taken account of the first point:

The alternative was that the Argentine may default. If a country defaults on all of its past debts, more money is released for the payment of future arms than would have been the case if she was held to repay her debts of the past. That is obvious.[28]

In other words, Mrs Thatcher was saying that a default would have shown clear foreign-exchange gains for the Argentinians.

Because the danger of default is real, the very threat of default is a powerful bargaining weapon in the hands of the debtors. As the economic and political pressures on them mount, they can be expected to insist with ever greater urgency that the banks bear their share of the burden of debt. Peru's President Garcia has charted one possible course. Argentina appeared, at the end of 1984 and the beginning of 1985, to be following another. It was reported to be nearly six months in arrears and still holding out for a better deal from the IMF, as it had the year before.[29] At the time of writing, Brazil too had declared that it would reach no new agreement with the IMF in 1985.[30] To the extent that the banks are forced to concede more 'new money' to offset the interest payments the debtors make in outstanding debt, the erosion of the credibility of bank balance sheets will continue. As we argue in the next chapter, that process of attrition entails costs not only for the banks but for the world economy as a whole. For the debtors the prospect is of bluffmanship which could too easily topple over into crisis and of sacrifices which offer no certain reward.

Western policy-makers should ask themselves whether the political and social systems of these countries can or should be made to take the strain. Venezuela and Mexico both have institutions which can, with a certain elasticity of language, be described as democratic. Both of the two other biggest debtors, Brazil and Argentina, began in 1983 and 1984 to emerge from a prolonged period of often brutally repressive military dictatorship. The new democratic politicians of these countries are being buffeted between two acute and conflicting pressures. On the one hand are the demands of the IMF and the banks to service their debt, on the other the rising expectations of a workforce whose real wages have plummeted and which wants to see a decisive break with the discredited policies of the previous military regimes. As a matter of policy, it seems foolish for the Western authorities to aggravate these conflicts at such a sensitive political moment in Latin America. But it is not even clear that if the West does continue to insist on debt service *à la* IMF, it will find itself with anything other than an economic crisis and political embarrassment. Political time horizons, in Latin America as elsewhere, are inevitably short. As Dr Henry

Kissinger summarized in a recent press commentary: 'Unfortunately, political leaders march to a different drummer than financial experts. They see the political interest of their country through the prism of their own survival. If pushed into a corner, a political leader may well seek to rally populist resentment against foreign "exploiters".' If pushed to make a choice between servicing the banks' debt and serving their people, few, if any, of Latin America's leaders are likely to fail to serve their people. Default cannot be ruled out on either economic or political grounds.

8

THE RISKS AND COSTS OF DOING NOTHING

The substitution of a credit mechanism in place
of hoarding would have repeated in the
international field the same miracle,
already performed in the domestic field,
of turning a stone into bread.

JOHN MAYNARD KEYNES
(*proposal for an International Clearing Union, April 1943*)

A default by one of the major borrowers or by a series of the smaller ones would have serious consequences not only for the Western banking system but for the world economy. One scenario was vividly painted by Mr Donald Regan, then the US Treasury Secretary, when arguing for an increase in the IMF's resources before the House Banking, Finance and Urban Affairs committee in December 1982. The statement is so clear, and sadly so little remembered or acted upon, that it is worth quoting *in extenso*:

The American citizen [Mr Regan said] has the right to ask why he and his government need to be concerned with debt problems abroad. With high unemployment at home, why should we be assisting other countries, rather than, say, reducing taxes or increasing spending domestically? Why should he care what happens to the international financial system?

One way to look at this question is to ask what the implications are for workers in Providence, Pascoag or Woonsocket if foreign borrowers do not receive sufficient assistance to adjust in an orderly way. What if they are late in making interest payments to banks, or can't pay principal, and loans become non-performing or are written off as a loss?

If interest payments are more than ninety days late, the banks stop accruing them on their books; they suffer reduced profits and bear the costs of continued funding of the loan. Provisions may have to be made for loss, and as loans are actually written off, the capital of the bank is reduced.

This in turn reduces the banks' capital/asset ratio, which forces banks to curtail lending to individual borrowers and lowers the overall total they can lend. The reduction in the amounts banks can lend will impact on the economy. So will the banks' reduced ability to make investments, which in everyday language includes the purchase of municipal bonds which help to finance the operations of the communities where individual Americans work and live. Reduced ability to lend could also raise interest rates.

I want to make very clear, Mr Chairman, that we are not talking here just about the big money-center banks and the multinational corporations. Well over 1,500 US banks, or more than 10 per cent of the total number of US banks, have loaned money to Latin America alone. They range in size from over $100 billion in assets to about $100 million. Those banks are located in virtually every state, in virtually every Congressional district, and in virtually every community of any size in the country. Those loans, among other things, financed exports, exports that resulted in jobs, housing and investment being maintained or created throughout the United States.

If the foreign borrowers are not able to service those loans, not only will US banks not be able to continue lending abroad, they will have to severely curtail their lending in the United States. Let me illustrate this point as graphically as I can. A sound, well run US bank of $10 billion in assets – not all that large today – might have capital of $600 million. It is required by the regulators to maintain the ratio of at least $6 in capital to every $100 in assets. What happens if 10 per cent, or $60 million, of its capital is eroded through foreign loan losses? It must contract its lending by $1 billion. Now realistically, the regulators will not force it to contract immediately, but they will force it to restrict its growth until its capital can be rebuilt.

The net result in either event is $1 billion in loans that can't be made in that community – 20,000 home mortgages at $50,000 each that can't be financed, or 10,000 lines of credit to local businesses at $100,000 each that can't be extended.

And of course, this reduction in lending will have negative effects on financing of exports, imports, domestic investment and production in individual cities and states around the United States, be it in shipping, tourist facilities, farming or manufacturing. The impact will not only be on the banks – it will negatively affect the individual as well as the economic system as a whole. Higher unemployment and a reduction in economic activity, with all they entail for city, state and Federal budgets, would be a further result. None of this is in the interest of the US citizen.[1]

A hypothetical illustration of the gravity of the problem can be seen from calculations of the consequences of Argentina, Mexico and Brazil missing *just one year's* payment of principal and interest, calculated on the basis of 1983 figures by Professor William Cline. If these countries were to miss their payments in such a clear-cut way that the banks were forced to write off that year's flow, the nine largest U S banks would have to lose 18 per cent of their capital simply because their profits from other loans would not be large enough to absorb all the loss. In order to re-establish the legally required ratio of capital to loans, they would have to cut back their loans by a multiple of the cut in their capital. Potentially the nine largest banks would have to cut their loans outstanding by approximately $160 billion as the result of a loss of $8 billion of their capital from one year's loss of the three countries' payments.[2]

If a default by major debtors suggested that the banks would be unable to recoup payments for the foreseeable future, it is hard to see how the regulators could do other than insist that the loans were written off in the banks' balance sheets. Even if, as a temporary measure, the regulators decided to relax capital requirements – a move which would look decidedly odd at a time when, if anything, the need for strong capital requirements was even greater – then it would still be unlikely that more than half of the big nine money-centre banks could be regarded as having more capital than the loans to be written off. The problem for these banks is that this would be far more serious than merely a liquidity crisis, in which the banks would still be basically sound but would have run short of cash. In a liquidity crisis a bank (at some cost) can go to the central bank as a lender of last resort and borrow the cash necessary to pay depositors, thus giving it time to call in its loans. But if a substantial part of the loans is worthless, the bank is simply insolvent. It needs a capital injection before it can sensibly continue trading.

Exactly this situation arose with the collapse of Continental Illinois, one of the nine biggest American money-centre banks. The immediate cause of its problems was a book of poor loans to American energy companies, but its enormous exposure to the developing-country debtors was the reason why it could not absorb the resulting losses or find a partner prepared to plough in the capital to do so. In Continental's case, it was simply too big and its assets too questionable for any other bank to be willing to swallow it. The same would happen in the case of the other money centres if they were brought down by Third World debt. No private-sector rescuer has both the resources and the expertise to step in and operate the business. Firms in industry with the necessary capital do not have the expertise. And other banks are by definition smaller and have their own problems. As in the Continental case, public authorities would have to step in with a capital injection. What is more, the size of the injections required would be such as to postpone indefinitely any hope that the big money centres could be easily floated off into the private sector once again in the short run. The effect would be to nationalize a large part of the American banking system. In Britain, the same situation would arise in the case of two of the biggest clearing banks, Lloyds and the Midland.

A back-door nationalization of the banks would be distinctly unwelcome to President Reagan and Prime Minister Thatcher, but in reality there would be little option if the biggest banks were to continue to operate and minimize the extent of the credit contraction. Smaller banks, of course, would also be affected by defaults, though not to the same degree. In their case some regulatory flexibility on capital requirements and a prolonged period of slow growth in their loan books might be enough to keep them out of the public sector and to rebuild their tattered balance sheets. However, that too would inevitably entail costs, as a slower growth of credit – both internationally and domestically – would be bound to have effects on economic activity and employment. A rescue operation could not isolate the real economy of output and jobs from the deep malaise of the financial sector.

The process sounds as if it might be handled smoothly, though the reality is that any solvency crisis would almost certainly be accompanied and aggravated by the more traditional liquidity crisis. As soon as a serious default became known, bank depositors would attempt to remove their money from the banks thought to be most at risk. Small depositors would have least to lose because in almost all states of the US accounts of up to $100,000 are guaranteed by the Federal Deposit Insurance Corporation (FDIC), a fact advertised at many tellers' windows. Nevertheless, there is a long history of small depositors panicking, the most recent instance of which, in Ohio in March 1985, forced the closure of seventy-one small savings and loan thrift institutions (the equivalent of Britain's building societies).[3] There is nothing like queues of savers stretching out of bank offices for providing alarming television pictures – and nothing more sure to extend the queues.

The main impact on the deposits of banks, though, would

come from the big depositors. Less than three-quarters of American deposits are guaranteed by the FDIC, and the holders of the remaining quarter could be expected to move fast.[4] Big depositors may have accounts linked directly with the interest rates that banks themselves pay on the wholesale market for deposits, or in the case of corporations they may themselves be lenders on the money markets via instruments like Certificates of Deposit. Their reaction would be to move their money from the afflicted banks into assets perceived to be safer, the most obvious alternative being short-term Federal government stock – Treasury bills. At the time of the Continental Illinois crisis, in the midsummer of 1984, the interest rates on big deposits in the money-centre banks stood 1.5 percentage points above the interest rate on three-month Treasury bills – treble the typical spread of about 0.5 per cent. Although that gap narrowed through the autumn of 1984, its responsiveness to any hint of a banking crisis was once again demonstrated in the spring of 1985, when the collapse of a small government securities firm in Florida – the fourth such failure since Drysdale Securities in 1982 – sent judders through the money markets. The classic response of the public in a bank run, however, is merely to hold cash, and it is this likely increase in the demand for money for purely precautionary reasons – as opposed to its use as a means of purchase – that would create most difficulties for central banks.

The Federal Reserve has been criticized for supplying inadequate amounts of cash to the banking system during the 1929 crash and thereby helping to cause the subsequent depression. In Europe there are critics of the Bank of England's handling of the secondary bank crisis in 1975 and of the Bundesbank's closure of Bank Herstatt in 1974. Certainly, the US Federal Reserve sailed triumphantly through the Continental Illinois crisis in the summer of 1984, the biggest banking débâcle it had had to deal with in a generation. There is inevitably, however, a question mark over the central banks' ability to handle a much larger crisis affecting many banks and their relationships with banks in other countries.

In the case of Continental Illinois, the Federal Reserve was able to stabilize the run on deposits – albeit with discount-window borrowing by the bank running at $6 billion a day at the peak of the crisis – largely by reshuffling money *between* the banks. Because the loss of confidence was restricted largely to

Continental Illinois, its fleeing depositors moved to other banks or into the Treasury bill market. The total cash reserves supplied to the banking system over the period of the crisis hardly changed, as the Fed. reined in from other banks cash which it supplied to Continental Illinois through the discount window.[5] The same trick would be infinitely more difficult to pull off if most of the money-centre banks were losing deposits quickly – and not just to other banks but to the proverbial bedsocks. A renewal of the debt crisis following serious defaults would take the world's financial system into waters thankfully uncharted since the 1930s.

Precisely because a major default would affect the whole of the international banking system rather than just one or two of its national constituent parts, it would also test the arrangements for supervising and providing lender-of-last-resort facilities to offshore and consortium banks. In theory, the Basle concordat of 1975 and its subsequent amendments have provided an international supervisory net. By implication there are also tacit arrangements between the central banks concerning their role as lenders of last resort – though it has been a deliberate policy of the central bankers to leave the extent and terms of such lending vague in order not to encourage 'imprudent lending'.[6] However, as we saw in Chapter 2, the European and Japanese banks' deposits in dollars enormously outweigh the dollar resources of their central banks, which would be unable to act as lenders of last resort. Their foreign-currency reserves would simply be inadequate, and the chances of arranging a large enough loan from the Federal Reserve system in the time available look remote. In Britain's case, the dollar deposits of the banks total $496 billion against Bank of England reserves worth $14 billion.[7]

A year before the Banco Ambrosiano collapse, W. P. Cooke, the head of banking supervision at the Bank of England, made one of those engaging admissions about official inadequacies that always carefully refer to some distant and inferior past, banished in favour of an unimprovable present:

Looking back, it is now clear that at the beginning of the 1970s the perceptions and techniques of the banking supervisory authorities had not kept pace with [internationalization]. There was, in effect, a supervisory vacuum in this new global market which needed to be filled. Neither the supervisors, nor indeed the banks themselves, had fully appreciated the degree to which the banking environment was changing in character and the new increased risks involved in international business.[8]

On the issue of dollar facilities for non-American banks, we will not know whether the banking supervisors have, like generals, been fighting the last war until a general crisis is upon us.

The influence of a serious default would extend to all other financial markets and into the real economy of output and jobs through other channels as well as the influence of a credit crunch. We have no faith in our, or anyone else's, ability to quantify the effects of a major default. It would be a leap into the unknowable in which uncertainty and doubt could have devastating effects. The extent to which confidence disintegrated would depend on whether other debtors swiftly followed the lead of the defaulter and on whether bank depositors anticipated a crash. The dislocation of the banking system would create a situation in which businesses would not know whose credit was good and whose bad. If the banks themselves were insolvent, whose credit could be trusted? Orders would go unfilled. Businesses would cut output and meet demand from stocks. Jobs could be lost by the hundreds of thousands.

One way of trying to provide quantitative answers about the effect of default is by using econometric models of the world economy, an exercise which was done in late 1984 by both of the biggest American forecasting groups, Data Resources, Inc. and Wharton Econometric Forecasting Associates.[9] Their results, like any such exercise, are subject to important caveats, full allowance for which would make a crisis far worse than they suggest. The first is that previously observed economic relationships would not hold in crisis circumstances. Secondly, even small changes in the key assumptions which both groups have to make now would generate very different results.

In both exercises one of the main deflationary forces operating on the world economy comes from cuts in Latin American imports. In reality, however, debtors default in the reasonable expectation that their growth will thereby be higher because the foreign exchange thus released will be able to increase the level of their imports and domestic output. However, both studies also assume (either implicitly or explicitly) that the Federal Reserve and other central banks would have considerable success in offsetting some of the more contractionary forces which could be triggered off by a default. As we have seen, those forces are likely to be far more uncontrollable and powerful than they suggest and would swamp any short-run increase in Latin American imports.

Once the depressive impact of contracting credit in the advanced countries made itself felt, it would be very difficult for the Latin Americans to maintain the same level of exports. They might therefore find themselves losing as much, if not more, foreign exchange than they might gain by refusing to continue full debt service. This point has been privately advanced by some senior officials in the industrial countries as a reason why default is unlikely. However, it fails to take account of the social, political or economic pressures on the debtors or the likelihood that defaults would occur gradually as one debtor after another was pushed to the brink. Each individual decision to default might be perfectly rational, even if the collective reality of successive defaults became a nightmare. During the Great Crash, Rothschilds no doubt thought that its withdrawal of support for the Creditanstalt would strengthen its own position, though the chain of collapses which it provoked almost certainly did the contrary.

The view is also based on a bizarre appraisal of the bargaining realities. In effect, the Western authorities are cast in the role of, say, a suicidal hijacker who is threatening to blow up an aircraft. The power of the hijacker rests wholly on the pilot's belief that he is prepared to destroy himself as well as everyone else. This is an unfortunate psychological analogy for the industrial countries, even if it were credible. It implies that the debtors who are required to make resource transfers to their creditors have a greater, or at least an equal, stake in the system as the creditors who receive them. In reality, the industrial countries have more to lose in a financial crisis than the defaulting debtors. The risks and dangers of default must inevitably be shared.

The present structure of world financial arrangements, while it continues, entails substantial risks but also exacts continuing costs from all the parties to it. In reality, the supposed transfer of financial resources from the debtors to the banks not only makes the debtors poorer – by a rather larger margin than the size of the transfers themselves, due to the multiplier effect from lower imports to national income – but also tends to *depress* the national income of the rich world. The idea that such financial flows benefit the industrial countries derives essentially from a false analogy with personal lending. Clearly, a lenders' income benefits when a borrower pays back the loan. But the process whereby these countries can repay loans is different. The only way they can find the foreign exchange to make the transfers is by increasing exports and cutting imports: that will involve, as it has in Latin America, a growth path permanently lower than would be the case if the loan were not being repaid (or were being funded by a further loan) in order to create large and permanent trade surpluses. But Latin America's trade surpluses must, by definition, be matched by industrial-country trade deficits. The process by which such deficits have increased has been in part through lower exports (particularly to Latin America) and in part through higher imports. Lower exports have cost the industrial countries jobs. To the extent that higher imports displace domestic production in the industrial countries rather than add to domestic income, they too cost output and jobs.

It could be argued that one way of avoiding this paradox whereby the repayment of international loans tends to make the lender poorer, is for the lender to increase domestic demand so as to absorb the extra imports and displaced exports without any loss to domestic production. At a time when most of the industrial countries have substantial surplus capacity of machinery and manpower, there are other sensible reasons for expanding domestic demand. However, most industrial-country governments – particularly the Europeans – have set their faces against any such expansion of demand on the grounds that they are afraid of rekindling inflation and that a good deal of such an increase would go on imports – presumably from such areas as Latin America.

Where the growth of domestic demand is effectively fixed by government policy, the increase in imports can come about only through an increase in debtors' market share and a fall in the market share of domestic producers. The increase in market share is attained by undercutting domestic goods and thereby increasing the real incomes of consumers in the rich countries.

But equally it displaces some of the producers in the rich countries, who become unemployed and endure a much lower income. The net effect, taken with the fall in exports, is certainly depressive: output and income, in aggregate, are lower in the rich countries. A further cost is a worsening of the distribution of income because the burden of the fall in output weighs on those industries which were previously exporting or competing with imports. The reaction is inevitably increasing protectionism, which is the way in which those people in the rich countries who are asked to bear this adjustment resist it. The process of attempting to be *rentier* economies, by extracting resource flows from these debtors, entails mutual deflation, which hurts the industrial countries and the developing countries alike.

Even if the advanced countries were to attempt to expand demand in order to accommodate the debtors' exports, they would have to be prepared for two consequences which history suggests they would resist. They would have to accept large and persistent trade deficits, when the repeated urge (notably in West Germany and Japan) has been the opposite. The experience of countries such as imperial Spain or Britain earlier this century, which did rely on *rentier* flows, is not likely to be persuasive. Secondly, it would still be unavoidable that some industries would lose jobs as a result of debtor competition. In principle, this consequence could eventually be offset by new jobs in other industries and services and be associated with a higher level of national income. But the new jobs would not necessarily be in the same place, or be available to the same skills, as the old ones. There would be at least a temporary increase in structural unemployment which would not be susceptible to cure by the expansion of demand. It is unlikely that advanced-country governments, already complaining that their high levels of unemployment are due to structural change, would be prepared to add to them.

The costs to the United States of the mistaken attempt to make the debtors pay the money back have been amply illustrated in a study published by the Federal Reserve Bank of New York.[10] The research calculates that the 40 per cent fall in American exports to Latin America between 1981 and 1983 caused the loss of nearly 250,000 U S jobs. This decline in exports was a brutal reversal in what had been one of the United States' fastest-growing export markets and one of the few areas of the world where it could count on running a substantial surplus in manufactures. Exports to Latin America accounted for only 17 per cent of total American exports in 1981, but they had been growing more than 50 per cent more quickly than US exports to the rest of the world.

The decline in exports hit particularly hard at many of the industries which were already experiencing difficulties because of the strength of the dollar. Exports of new cars and trucks fell by more than half in 1982. Basic iron and steel products and farm goods also halved. More than three-quarters of the estimated loss of about 225,000 jobs in 1982, due to a reduction of nearly $9 billion in merchandise exports, was attributed to the machinery, transport equipment and other manufacturing industries where unemployment was already higher than the US average. The study put the direct cut in American real GNP at 0.3 per cent (worth around $10 billion) before any further effects due to the reduced spending of those made unemployed and the reduction in investment of the companies whose profits were hit.

What is more, the study was confined to the early impact of debtor-country surpluses on the US, when the effect was merely the cut in Latin American imports. As Latin American exports built up in 1983 and 1984, there will have been additional costs to industries competing with those imports. These effects are not temporary ones, any more than the effect on the growth path of Latin America is temporary. *Growth* may conceivably resume its previous annual rates, but it will be from a lower base as a result of the debt crisis. It cannot be taken as an article of faith that the level of output which would otherwise have been attained will be reached unless the pressures contingent on Latin America's need to generate trade surpluses relent.

There are other costs inherent in the policy which the industrial countries have chosen to pursue in the debt crisis. The uncertainty which attaches to the prospects for the banks must alter behaviour. Indeed, it is possible that we are already paying some of the costs of a crisis because of anticipation on the part of many economic actors. This is particularly clear in the large discounts to book value which are available on bank shares. The uncertain nature of much of the banks' loans must also make them far more cautious about extending credit than they would otherwise have been as they attempt to build up capital ratios.

The new caution in bank lending is particularly noticeable with international loans: net international bank credit grew by only 7 per cent in 1984, with the lion's share of the growth going to the BIS's reporting area – in other words, the developed world. The Third World had an increase in credit outstanding of only 3 per cent, an amount of net 'new money' which, as we have seen, was not enough to offset the interest payments in the other direction. In the first quarter of 1985 outstanding credit to the non-reporting area actually fell.[11] Reverse flows are inevitably depressing Third World imports and world trade below the point at which they would otherwise be.

The outstanding stock of Third World debt has thus become a dead weight on economic activity, ensuring a deflationary bias to the world economy which the developed countries have so far been unprepared to lift through other means. When the growth of the stock of debt made it incredible that the servicing burden on the Third World could be sustained, the credit dried up – at exactly the time that higher interest rates and oil prices, together with stagnant export markets, implied all the greater need for current-account financing. The burden of reducing those deficits in line with available finance fell entirely on to the Third World: once again it was the deficit countries that were forced to adjust rather than those with surpluses. The result has been to drive down the level of world income and output in order to achieve payments balance. The debtors have paid most heavily for the crisis, but no one has gained.

9

TOWARDS REFORM

Some paradox of our nature leads us,
when once we have made our fellow men the objects
of our enlightened interest, to go on to make them
the objects of our pity, then of our wisdom,
ultimately of our coercion.

LIONEL TRILLING

In this final chapter we draw the strands of the argument together and set out some criteria for a solution to the debt problem. We look briefly at some of the proposals which have been advanced and explain what we believe to be their shortcomings. Finally, we outline our own preferred proposals for dealing with the crisis and meet some of the more prevalent objections to them.

Perhaps the most crucial perception to bear in mind is that until the first oil shock of 1973–4, the flows of funds to the developing countries were dominated, for the best of reasons, by officially controlled and provided finance. It was almost universally recognized among officials and bankers in the advanced countries that the requirements of the developing world could not be met effectively or safely within the framework of purely commercial finance.

After the 1973–4 oil shock the developing world's need for finance was even greater. The flows of lending fulfilled a vital role for developing and advanced countries alike. Without them the world economy would have deteriorated more swiftly and more gravely. However, the means by which those flows were channelled – overwhelmingly through the private banking systems of the advanced countries – were fraught with danger from the start, and owed more to expediency and an evasion of political responsibility than to sound policy.

If the official analysis of the unsuitability of private channels for development finance was correct in the relatively untroubled environment which prevailed before the 1973–4 oil shock, as we believe, then it should have carried even more force and weight in the turbulent circumstances of the 1970s, when the need for finance was even greater. Instead the unceasing search for the soft option led officials and politicians in all the advanced countries to encourage an exposed and vulnerable part of their financial and economic systems to bear a load which could properly and safely only be borne if supported by the community as a whole. Today's crisis stems above all from the decision to push private finance into fulfilling public purposes for which it was profoundly ill-suited.

It is thus essential to draw a clear distinction between the desirability of the flows of funds which did occur and the means used to assure them. We have seen that for much of the 1970s the flows of funds to the developing world enabled it to maintain relatively high rates of growth. This was to the benefit not only of its development but of world trade and the advanced countries as well. Such flows of finance have an impeccable rationale in economic theory, since they allow world output to be higher and to be produced more efficiently than would otherwise be the case. In this sense, the growth of commercial bank lending during the 1970s was a response – however ill thought out – to the lack of any mechanism in the international monetary system akin to Lord Keynes's proposal for an International Clearing Union which would be able to provide extended credit to ensure that balance-of-payments difficulties never caused world instability or deflation.

With some demonstrable exceptions, the flows of funds to the developing world during the 1970s were fruitful and were not, overall, excessive. The ratio of total debt to exports, for example, was not higher even in the most indebted countries than had historically been the case with some of today's developed countries which were at one time large net importers of capital, such as Canada, Australia and the United States. Nor, for much of the 1970s, were the terms of that borrowing onerous. But neither the authorities nor the bankers appear to have understood that this was a very different situation. In this case poor countries with large and growing populations were involved in lending on such a scale that the dominant role of the banks in the lending meant that the time required for service and repayment would inevitably lead to difficulties. As long as the growth in world trade was strong and normal conditions prevailed in the money markets, it did not require any effort of debt service on the part of the borrowers, since enough 'new money' was forthcoming to meet old repayments, interest on old debt and a margin in addition. The problems suffered subsequently, when interest rates rose and the recession began to bite, merely accelerated the decline of confidence which would have occurred at some point in any event as changed circumstances or the growing mountain of debt finally eroded belief that the snowball could continue.

The banks were never able to impose conditions on borrowers, so that in some cases lending was not used wisely and in others it was flagrantly misspent. The commercial maturities which the banks imposed did not, and do not, tally with the prolonged period which it was reasonable to suppose that many of the developing countries needed before they could sensibly be asked to become exporters of capital. The deliberate shifting of the interest-rate risk from lenders to borrowers made the debt vulnerable to any period of high interest rates. When confidence finally evaporated, the commercial banks displayed all the same 'boom-and-bust' symptoms which have become familiar in some other financial markets. The source of lending dried up precipitately at exactly the time when it was most needed to sustain world economic activity in the wake of the second oil shock. The crucial reason for the emphasis before 1973–4 on public finance was apparent; public authorities always can – and often do – reschedule official lending to the developing world without damage to their own financial stability. By contrast, the banks can engage in the same necessary exercise only at the cost of the increasing incredibility of their own balance sheets and the increasing risk of a steady loss of depositor confidence, which could undermine an essential part of the advanced countries' financial system.

The stock of debt now outstanding entails serious costs and risks for the world economy. It is supported on a shaky tripod of IMF programmes, export surpluses in the debtor countries and involuntary lending by the commercial banks. Neither the willingness of the debtor countries to run export surpluses nor the willingness of many banks to extend even limited amounts of new credit to offset a part of the reverse net transfers from debtors to creditors can sensibly be expected to withstand critical appraisal. The present reverse transfers are a wholly unintended result of stabilizing the world economy during the 1970s. Even without shocks to the world economy, the debtors face growing internal political pressure to discontinue the full service of their debt, since there is no realistic prospect that the commercial banks will resume lending on a scale sufficient to ensure that 'new money' fully offsets, let alone exceeds, debt-service payments. There remains, therefore, the potential for a serious banking crisis which would entail the effective nationalization of many of the advanced countries' largest banks and a spiral of contracting credit, defaults and recession which could too easily become a gruesome repeat of the 1930s.

This unhealthy situation is imposing costs on debtor and creditor countries alike, despite the avoidance so far of a widespread calamity. The caution now inevitably displayed by the banking system in its lending is a depressive force driving both Third World and advanced countries' output below where it would otherwise be. The effort to receive debt repayments from the developing world in the only way it can conceivably pay – through the generation of large trading surpluses – implies a process of adjustment on the part of the creditor countries as well, which must prove able and willing to accept their debtors' goods and services.

In theory, this 'repayment' can be in addition to goods and services provided at home and can therefore add to the income of the advanced countries without increasing their output. In reality, the anti-inflationary policies which most of them are currently pursuing imply that such debtor exports to the advanced countries replace domestic output and employment in those industries which compete directly. Protectionism is steadily increasing, in part because the pressure for debt service in turn is causing higher Third World exports and greater producer-group resistance in the industrial countries. Barter trade is replacing more orthodox and efficient forms of exchange. The contraction of the dollar banking system's new lending, not just to the debtor countries but around the world, is also perpetuating the grotesque misalignment of the American dollar and adding a further twist to the forced erosion of the liberal world trading order. There could hardly be a clearer case for change, since almost every participant in this sorry melodrama of the international financial system is losing from it.

The effort to justify these extraordinary results of the policies pursued since the first oil shock has led to embarrassing intellectual somersaults on the part of bankers and advanced-country officials, whose predecessors until 1982 would never have dreamed that the debtor developing countries should be asked to make transfers of resources to their creditors so soon or at such a low relative level of income. The implicit assumption of the lending banks through the 1970s was that there would always be some banks – if not themselves – prepared to refinance obligations coming due, so that the ultimate process of repaying debt would be postponed until the debtor countries were clearly prosperous enough to be able to do so. None of the bankers would have argued – and it is in reality impossible to do so today – that the time for repayment is now. For officials, the bank lending of the 1970s was merely a welcome and politically expedient extension of the governmental transfers to the developing world which had dominated the pre-oil shock phase and which had always been posited on the traditional tenets of development finance that did not assume early repayment or, indeed, repayment at all.

This view never entailed an appeal merely to *noblesse oblige* on the part of the advanced countries; positive transfers to the developing world were expected to fill a role in aiding their progress, and this was in the interests of the advanced countries as well. The world's economic activity is not a fixed whole, a larger slice of which for one country implies a smaller one for another. International co-operation, including these positive financial transfers to poorer nations, has clearly enabled the sum of world output to be higher than it would otherwise have been, without corresponding losses on the part of the rich nations.

The clearest example of this was the large programme of financial flows to Europe after the Second World War to aid its economic reconstruction. The lessons of German reparations after the First World War had been learned. Between 1949 and 1952 the United States transferred the equivalent of 4.5 per cent of its GNP in Marshall Aid, the largest instance of sustained international financial flows in history. Yet far from reducing the USA's level of national income, even a cursory glance at its national accounts shows an acceleration of growth and of personal incomes during the period. The Marshall plan was certainly generous, but it involved an enlightened and self-interested generosity; as a result, the USA once again had a trading partner and competitor which ensured both that the level of world trade was given a substantial fillip and that there were positive welfare gains through greater choice and competition. Both Europe and the USA benefited.

It is sometimes argued that there can be no parallel between war-ravaged Europe and the countries of the developing world today because of the latter's lack of human skills or spare production capacity. For this reason the parallel with the poorest countries of the world can certainly not be pushed too far. However, the Latin American economies are endowed with a relatively skilled and educated population. Moreover, these countries have already shown that they will be capable of much higher rates of economic growth than they are currently achieving when the key constraints on their progress are lifted. Clearly, a large number of those obstacles are domestic and can be relieved only through policies which ensure that markets are allowed to work properly (where they do work) and that sound financial policies keep inflation at bay. However, an external constraint is also imposed on these economies through the lack of foreign exchange, which can in turn be relieved by the action of the creditor countries. Some economists have argued that positive financial flows to the developing world have been wasted and, in some cases, have impeded development. Even these thinkers, however, have yet to argue that a financial flow from the developing world to its richer creditors is beneficial to their growth. No school of economic thought argues other than that the negative financial flows to the advanced countries are an aberration which should be ended swiftly.

The first criterion for any reform must therefore be that it is adequate in its scope to end the negative flows from the Third World to the industrial countries. Without some means of ensuring that the debtor countries become net recipients of funds, the deflationary impact of their outstanding debt cannot easily be remedied. At the same time, a reversal of the flows is the only long-term guarantee that a co-operative solution can be reached between debtor and creditor countries, and this is a necessary condition of the long-term safety of the Western banking system. The banks must have time – perhaps more than a decade – to make the necessary write-offs of the present debts out of profits, without excessive impairment of their capital and hence their ability to lend. At the very least, the present negative transfers, with their attendant requirement of substantial Third World trade surpluses, must be neutralized.

The second criterion is that any 'new money' over and above that required to neutralize present interest payments should be used, in so far as this can be guaranteed, to build up the productive capacity of the borrowing countries, and particularly their capacity to earn foreign exchange. This criterion implies that in the developing countries the present institutions for the allocation of lending must be more heavily involved in determining the use of 'new money' made available by the international system, for only then can there be reasonable assurance that normal criteria within the country are being applied to the proposed projects. The banks in the developing countries should remain the main point of distribution and allocation, which in turn points strongly to the desirability of the commercial banks continuing to have a large role in extending funds. In some cases, such as Citibank's large subsidiary in Brazil, there is a direct link between a Western bank and the banking system of a developing country. In others there is a fairly long history of association and expertise. An additional advantage of using the commercial banking system as the conduit for flows is that it avoids the politically problematic course of almost any alternative. If the commercial banks can be encouraged to extend their lending, the flows of funds will not register as a charge on national exchequers, taxes and borrowing requirements.

The third criterion, intimately related to the second, is that a system of regulation must govern commercial banking flows. Without a structure in which the commercial banks can operate, new lending would be subject to all the foibles and follies of the past. In the aggregate, the likelihood would be that periods of feast would be succeeded by equally pronounced periods of fast, ensuring that the commercial banking system acted as a destabilizing element of the world monetary system rather than as a productive and balancing factor leaning against the world trade cycle. In individual cases regulation is also required to stop over-borrowing and to ensure that the unspecific nature of foreign-currency finance, which is difficult to tie down to particular uses, is not exploited for the prosecution of megalomaniac projects. This inevitably implies that individual countries should have outline targets for foreign-currency finance and that a system of incentives and disincentives should be put in place to assure that they are met. It also implies that those targets should be conditional on the pursuit of sensible domestic economic policies.

Most of the proposals for changes in the present arrangements that are current in official circles in the advanced countries fail one or other of these criteria.[1] The industrial countries' governments are still clearly hoping that a patchwork approach of small changes will suffice. A classic example is the offer made at the London summit in 1984 to encourage Multi-Year Rescheduling Arrangements (MYRAs) instead of the prevalent annual reschedulings of debt coming due each year. Under the MYRAs signed by several of the debtor countries – notably Mexico in September 1984 – the creditor banks have agreed to reschedule debt coming due in future years as well, so ensuring that one year's rescheduling does not merely aggravate the problems of a further rescheduling a couple of years hence. The advantages of this practice are not only that, in theory anyway, large humps of debt repayments can be smoothed over but also that the arduous, time-consuming and irritating process of annual reschedulings can be ended. A properly negotiated MYRA also clearly has the potential to spread out a given expected net transfer from a debtor country to creditor countries. What it cannot do, however, is change the reality of an expected reverse transfer. The debtor merely exchanges what may be a period of acute hardship for a longer and more enervating period in which the transfers, in total, are expected to be the same (or, indeed, larger to take account of the interest required on deferred repayments). The central aberration of the debt crisis – the reverse transfer – would continue, albeit in less acute and more prolonged form.

The same criticism applies to other schemes which aim to link debt service with particular economic conditions, postponing payments when times are bad and recouping them when they improve, though at least the reverse transfers would be regulated according to some notion of ability to pay rather than, as with MYRAs, merely stretched out arbitrarily. Such schemes could operate either on repayments of principal or on interest. The first type would incorporate 'bisque' clauses linking repayments of principal to the fulfilment of particular targets such as export growth. Schemes proposing measures to spread out the impact of high interest rates have been more popular; a specific interest-rate cap has been suggested by Mr

Anthony Solomon, until recently the head of the Federal Reserve Bank of New York. Under this proposal, a cap would be set on interest rates so that any excess of the market rate over the cap would be rolled into future debt and repaid when the market interest rate once again subsided below the cap.

A similar idea would be to extend the IMF's Compensatory Financing Facility (CFF), which currently provides some compensation for developing countries which suffer a sharp fall in the price of their main commodity exports. The CFF could cover variable interest rates as well. Clearly, the interest-rate cap, or the rate for which debtors were compensated by the IMF, could in principle be set at such a level as to have the effect of cancelling out reverse transfers. This, nevertheless, seems a roundabout way of tackling a problem which arises not only from the obligations on the existing stock of debt but also from the lack of new lending. It also seems far from the intentions of the proposers. Moreover, most of these schemes are incompatible with unsupported private finance. They require budgetary support from governments.

Various other ideas have been mooted which are not necessarily tied to a solution of the debt crisis but which would clearly have some beneficial effects. The World Bank's project financing and its structural-adjustment loans both have a useful role to play in development finance, and the quality of the institution's lending is much admired. One important way of bridging the financing gap for many Third World countries, particularly the poorest, would be to enlarge the scope of the World Bank's financing by allowing it to raise more money on international capital markets.

Its present borrowings could quickly be doubled, without appealing for capital from its member countries, which would have to be voted by national parliaments. The highly conservative 1:1 ratio of capital to lending which is currently insisted upon could be eased. It is far-fetched to argue that such an expansion would either reduce the credit standing of the institution or impose strains on domestic capital markets by 'crowding out' other borrowers. The World Bank raised only $11 billion on world capital markets in fiscal 1985 and took care to spread its liabilities in different currencies and capital markets.

There is also a strong case, only partially linked to the debt crisis, for a further issue to all members of the IMF's own 'currency', the Special Drawing Right (SDR). The SDR, to all intents an international reserve currency recognized by IMF members as equivalent to, say, the dollar or the Deutschmark, has an important part to play in increasing international liquidity, where it is needed. A fresh issue would enable many IMF members to meet a part of their debt obligations by what amounts to an increase in the world money supply.

Such an increase is more likely to stimulate output than inflation precisely because of the relatively high levels of spare capacity in the world economy. The extent of any SDR issue, however, is likely to make it of only marginal importance in negating the reverse transfers from the developing countries, since issues have tended in the past to be in proportion to the IMF member countries' quota subscriptions to the Fund and hence broadly to their economic weight. An interesting variation on the usual SDR issue, proposed by Mr Nathaniel Samuel, would be to make the new issue available to the Fund itself as a form of its own resources which it would be able to disburse to countries undergoing adjustment programmes. This would ensure that the SDR allocation tended to go where it was needed and at the same time provide the IMF with an incentive to impose less stringent and depressive lending conditions, which are implicitly justified only because the Fund has relatively scarce resources for lending.

An expansion of World Bank and IMF resources would be of particular use in easing any future adjustments to new world economic shocks but would be unlikely to be adequate to provide for the developing world's continuing and regular need for balance-of-payments finance. A more thoroughgoing reform is also required to deal with the debt crisis and to set in place a long-term and sustainable system of financial flows.

Many of the more radical proposals specifically designed to alleviate the debt crisis concentrate on eliminating the 'debt overhang' of outstanding obligations. The method favoured by most of the influential proponents of these ideas (notably Mr Felix Rohatyn, who was largely responsible for saving New York City from bankruptcy, or Peter B. Kenen of Princeton, Senator Bill Bradley and Congressman Charles E. Schumer)[2] is some form of discounting of the debt on the banks' books.

This would take the form, say, of a new agency which would buy up developing-country debt held by the banks at a discount of 10 per cent (or more) of its face value, paying the banks in long-term bonds against itself and in turn becoming the creditor of the developing countries. The agency would be able to grant some debt relief (made available by the discount) and stretch the maturities of the loans to provide more comfortable repayment schedules. The banks would have a more secure, governmentally guaranteed asset on their books, though they would also, of course, have to accept losses to the extent that the loans were discounted.

A more extreme solution to the problem of the 'debt overhang' has been supported by Professor Milton Friedman and others.[3] Their 'market-solution' would be to force the banks to price the worth of their developing-country debt in the marketplace, which would determine its value. They would then be required to write down losses according to the value placed on the assets by the market. The theory is that the debt of countries which are heavy borrowers would trade at a larger discount, ensuring high enough rates of interest to discourage them from borrowing any more. Indeed, such advocates of the 'market solution' would dispense with the role of IMF conditionality altogether, allowing the marketplace to decide what the conditions for new borrowing would be.

In the real world any such change would almost certainly provoke the very crisis it is designed to cure. Any secondary market which effectively made bank debt into traded bonds would rapidly show such large discounts on the debt of some of the big borrowers as to call into question the solvency of debtors and banks. A debtor faced with extremely high interest rates on any new borrowing would probably not only stop borrowing but default on past debt as well. After all, the strongest incentive to the borrowers to continue to service their debt is the hope and expectation that the anomaly of reverse transfers will somehow be brought to an end. A change which effectively put paid to any such prospect would also be likely to put an end to continued debt service.

Apart from the effect on banks' balance sheets, this is also an objection to the proposals for any form of international debt-discounting agency. In effect, debt-discounting might deal with the problem of the 'debt overhang' but at the cost of aggravating the problem of extending 'new money'. Which of the banks selling present Third World debt to such an agency, at a forced discount and a substantial loss, is going to be willing to extend further funds to the indebted countries? The agency and its discounts would be a continuing and sharp reproof to any director on the board of a major bank who proposed new lending to one of the debtors whose previous obligations had been treated in this manner. Though the present problems of the lending banks might be resolved at some cost to them, a further result would almost certainly be to leave the discounting agency – and the taxpayer – with a great deal of defaulted and worthless debt.

All the discounting proposals, indeed, skirt around this central problem, in that they merely shift what is likely to become a heavier burden as a result of the discounting. The question is not merely how to give the banks' balance sheets some semblance of financial rectitude but also how to ensure new flows of money to the developing world. The two cannot be easily separated, since a solution which tackles only one side of the problem is likely to leave the other side even more intractable. And if the new flows are not assured, much of the existing debt, whoever holds it, is likely to become worthless.

Any sensible reform of existing arrangements must, as a minimum requirement, bring to an end the reverse transfer from the developing countries which now covers part of the interest payments on existing bank debt. It must also deal with the problem of the existing debt on the banks' books. If, on the one hand, the debtors are to be relieved of negative transfers in the years immediately ahead and, on the other hand, the bank debts are to remain 'performing' (i.e. with current interest up to date), that interest must be financed by new lending. It is wholly unrealistic to suppose that this will be achieved voluntarily in the coming years without some form of reliable guarantee. The governments of the advanced countries must provide this guarantee through their institutions in order to ensure the necessary flow of lending. The chronic danger that existing debts will become 'non-performing' for lack of current interest payments will be brought to an end. These interest payments would no longer be dangerously and undesirably dependent on the debtor countries' continuous achievement of an export surplus.

The guarantee would be made dependent upon the agreement of the banks that they would each year write down, according to circumstances, that part of their existing debt which was judged bad or doubtful. It would also require their agreement to long-term rescheduling of the interest on that part of the debt that was written down. That vicarious guarantee, however, would give the banks many years to write off old debt on their balance sheets without excessively impairing their profitability, capital position or ability to lend.

The key to achieving new bank lending would be a form of insurance akin to the export credit guarantee schemes operating in most advanced countries. Under these schemes exporters are insured so that they are paid even if they are unable to collect debts for exports. But it is not their practice to insure the foreign-currency lending needed to make debt payments. The institutions which could guarantee new bank lending are already in place – for example, the Export-Import Bank in the United States and the Export Credit Guarantee Department in the United Kingdom.

At first the amounts of guaranteed new lending would have to be large enough to offset the present reverse transfers – probably of the order of $30–40 billion. However, this is lending which would be met not by public budgets or borrowing requirements but by commercial credit. There would be a long-term contingent liability on the guarantor in respect of any ultimate failure to pay. The amount involved, though large, is small relative to the increases in credit during the 1970s and even smaller compared with the $8,000 billion annual output of the advanced countries. After all, even one year's normal growth in this output is worth $300 billion. The amounts guaranteed each year would dwindle as the banks gradually wrote off old debt, thereby also reducing the immediate burden of interest to the borrowers.

The guarantees would be given upon the advice of the IMF, which would set annual ceilings of guaranteed 'new money', case by case, for each of the debtor countries. It would take account of the estimated reverse transfer in each case, and further lending would be conditional on economic policies (agreed between the IMF and the debtors) designed to foster the growth of investment and living standards. This would require a radical revision of the IMF's operating mandate. The key difference between this conditionality and the Fund's present rules is that conditions would be designed to justify and ensure transfers to the developing world so that it can cover its debt interest rather than to extract transfers from it. This would bring to an end the present basic conflict between the IMF's purposes and those of the developing countries themselves.

Certainly, domestic policies of the debtors would have to be shown to be sound, even austere. But they would be part of a workable package designed to relieve the foreign-exchange constraint on developing-country growth. Some argue that this type of conditionality would be an intrusion on the sovereignty of the debtors. However, any advanced country committed to promoting growth and rising living standards should not be required to underwrite mistaken policies, such as over-valued exchange rates for the benefit of an import spree or capital flight, nor to underwrite the military adventures of an irresponsible junta. It is in the borrower's long-term interest too when a lender seeks to ensure that the credit extended will be used for sound purposes. Any public lender must be doubly sure in order to attract backing at home.

The guarantee of this lending would ensure that the finest terms would be obtained by the debtors. The administration of the guarantee could be in the hands of national export credit agencies and would ensure that proposed loans fell within the envelope set year by year by the IMF. Under the guarantee the ultimate liability for any failed loans could be borne by the advanced countries as a whole, through the IMF. This guarantee scheme would be based on the assumption that there could be no firmly predictable time when it would be right and proper to seek service from the debtors, whose circumstances will doubtless vary. It is possible that some of the countries which have shown most dramatic and successful growth over the last two decades – notably Taiwan and South Korea – will, in a decade or two, be able and willing to become net capital exporters rather than importers. But no date can be set for any country whose standard of living is still a fraction of that of the advanced countries. The advanced countries must be prepared to fund this part of the debtors' balance-of-payments requirements through officially underwritten guarantees without specific time limits. This is no more nor less than the explicit assumptions made during the 1960s about official aid and lending, and during the 1970s by the bankers, who always expected that they or other banks would be prepared to roll over the debt until the point at which the development of the debtor was assured enough for it to embark on repayments. It made sense then, and does so now.

One advantage of the scheme is that it would allow the IMF and the banks together to fulfil the role of a properly functioning international credit market, particularly in times of severe world disturbance to balance-of-payments equilibria. The overall size of the cumulated debtor-country 'envelopes' could be varied in some degree according to the international environment, expanding, for example, in the wake of an oil shock to allow greater time for adjustment without loss of output and a decline in living standards. Similarly, the 'envelopes' could be contracted at a time of rising world inflation. In our view, it would be reasonable to extend the guarantee beyond its minimum purpose of ending negative interest payments to the provision of further 'new money' to the debtors. Whether this would be acceptable, and in what amounts, would be a matter for judgement and agreement by the advanced countries' governments.

This is part of the riposte to any suggestion that such a scheme might prove to be inflationary if excessive credit-financed payments deficits were allowed. The extent of the guarantees would depend on circumstance and could be used to counter either excessive deflation or inflation. No one suggested, in the wake of the first oil shock, that the unregulated bank lending to the developing countries was inflationary. Indeed, a chorus of voices urged more lending to avert the risk of a prolonged depression. It ill behoves many of the same analysts and politicians now to argue that any regulated scheme, well founded on an appreciation of the real constraints on growth in the debtor countries and the world economy, would be inflationary. Indeed, the more stable environment offered by such guarantees might well encourage more stable prices, particularly if investment in debtor countries' commodity exports were stimulated as a result. A greater assurance of supply of key commodities would inevitably entail a lesser risk of an inflationary shock of the 1972–3 variety from the commodity markets.

One final class of objection, particularly popular in more rarefied academic circles, is that any attempt to place the 'debt overhang' on a sound basis would merely encourage the banks to expose themselves in future to greater risks on the supposition that they would be once again bailed out. This so-called problem of 'moral hazard' could scarcely be less apposite in current circumstances or in criticism of the scheme we have outlined. The moral hazard is relevant when considering individual loans but has no bearing on lending when the risks and purposes of the lending are appraised, approved and supervised by public authority.

In any event, the problem is, after all, not to persuade the banks to avoid excessive risks in their sovereign lending but to persuade them to undertake any lending at all. The experience of the years since the Mexican crisis in 1982 has left many bankers so scared that the collective fear of any such escapade is likely to endure for a very long time, which is precisely why we are confident in asserting that the resumption of voluntary, unsupported, international bank lending is unlikely to begin again in the foreseeable future. Any lending outside the guarantee would be covered by normal regulatory procedures.

The effect of all this would be that the banks would be given time to write off gradually a good deal of the outstanding debt of the major developing countries. This lengthy process could be assured only if the debtors had an interest in preserving the proper functioning of the international system and avoiding unilateral action which could provoke a crisis. The debt crisis is a banking crisis and a crisis of developing-country growth. Action on the lines we propose would mean that, for the first time, public purpose and private banking finance would be working in a sustainable partnership to deal with the problem.

The present adjustment process is fundamentally defective because it is centrally related to the debtors' capacity to achieve the premature and undesirable export surpluses needed to transfer resources to the advanced countries. It leaves the debtors and the bankers in a state of chronic fragility. It repudiates the sound principles and purposes which caused governments to encourage this lending in the first place. The present adjustment process impedes growth and spurs inflation. It dangerously aggravates the political tensions, domestic and international, of both creditor and debtor nations.

There are many different ways of resolving this problem. The details of a new reform are less important than the mustering of political will in the advanced countries to change a perilous and unsustainable situation. The political pressures which the debtors currently face, having lost what may amount to a decade of development as a result of the mismanagement of the reaction to the shocks of the 1970s, should not be underestimated. The volcano of the debt crisis is dormant but far from extinct. The authorities of the advanced countries have little time in which to ensure that it does not once again heave and erupt. At stake are not merely the well-being of the populations of the debtor countries but the living standards of each and every nation that is reliant for its prosperity on the health of the world's trading and financial system.

10

POSTSCRIPT TO THE AMERICAN EDITION

We have argued in this book that the international debt crisis can be solved only by co-operative effort between banks, governments, international institutions and the debtor countries. The debt question is, in truth, as indicated in the Preface, formed of a trinity of economic issues where the world has lost its way: trading arrangements, parity management and trade deficits.

1. Trading Arrangements

The idea of liberalisation of trade greatly encouraged post-war inter-dependence. It was rightly seen that the world's wealth would be increased by the stimulus to the international division of labor, that the poorer countries would develop and innovation and adaptation would flourish in the developed areas. GATT was set up to regulate and sustain the freer trade. Both the philosophy which inspired GATT and the mechanisms on which it relied were initially rather vague and incomplete, perhaps inevitably. Everybody was in favor of more free trade, but little thought was given to the pace at which domestic production could be replaced by imports or to the disruption this would cause. There was little attempt, in either government or academic circles, to elucidate or appraise the hard political and economic difficulties likely to emerge, still less to expound a coherent set of principles to apply when they did. The accelerating rush to protectionism in the last ten to fifteen years has cruelly underlined this truth. The world is now exposed to the dangers of trade war with insufficient intellectual armoury. The cry of 'lost jobs' and a political reaction to it was no doubt inevitable. But there is also analytical confusion. Instead of an overwhelming consensus to sustain freer trade there is now philosophic advocacy, from reputable quarters, of the regression to protectionism. There are attempts, even, to articulate a philosophy which will justify further regression. Not for the first time, some of our academics have proved only too ready to produce theoretical support for the least justifiable impulses of government.

2. Parity Management

The consensus in favor of free trade was rightly supported by a recognition that it required reasonably stable exchange rates. Yet when the Bretton Woods system appeared to require modernisation, the leading countries of the world precipitately abandoned it. We needed to deal with the inability of the United States to influence its own parity or to cover its external monetary imbalances by gold payments. Instead, the world's leaders opted for floating rates, while still pledging themselves 'in full co-operation with the International Monetary Fund and those who trade with us to press for the necessary reforms to set up an urgently needed new international monetary system.' The pledge confirms that there was no agreed sense among governments that floating rates provided a basis for a superior monetary system. But nothing was done. The pledge continues to be unredeemed. International money power has passed into the hands of international restlessness.

In theory, the move to floating rates took place without abandoning the commitment to international co-operation either in regulating parities or in liberalising trade. The apostles of floating failed to anticipate that violent swings in parity would result or that trade patterns and capital movements would become dominated by monetary fluctuations rather than by comparative economic advantage. They failed to see that the underlying rationale of a liberal trade and investment order had been undermined.

The assertion that during this period we have suffered from major deformities in exchange rates will be challenged by some, but not now by very many. The intellectual bandwagon in favour of floating brushed aside those who expressed anxiety that there would be a dangerous weakening of the influence of fundamental economic factors of growth, productivity and price levels. Many, more familiar with the realities of markets than with the exercises of the seminar, warned that major and prolonged anomalies in parity would occur – that the immediate ebb and flow of capital movements, often purely money and banking movements, would overwhelmingly determine parities. Even when real life demolished the optimistic theorists of the floating rate, those of them who were genuinely anti-protectionist continued, surprisingly, to ignore the threat to liberal trade from deformed parities.

Monetary instability continues to weaken the whole fabric of post-war achievement. What now of the claim that free-floating rates would act as automatic pilot to steer countries away from unmanaged trade balances? Vastly greater and more anomalous imbalances have been produced in trading and current accounts. Dangerous inadequacies in their financing abound and they imperil the banking system, the debtors and world trade.

The three great motivations of governments, and the academic theorists who spurred them on, were that floating rates would give governments greater say in running their own economies, that the dollar would be dethroned as the predominant world currency, and that speculation in the currency markets would have less scope. All three motivations were fantasies. Floating rates brought new restrictions to domestic policy because their volatility had immense repercussions on inflation and the pattern of trade and production. The formal dethronement of the dollar in many respects increased its predominance, as well as removing restraints which had previously prevented temporary swings in dollar movements from automatically dislocating the parities of other countries. Floating rates did not reduce the power of the giant. They turned it loose.

For the same reason, far from ending speculation, free floating multiplied it. We have got to a point where daily transactions in currencies exceed fifty times the amount required for world trade and investment. What a misallocation of human energy and ingenuity! Nor, as was often claimed by the theorists, has this speculation dampened currency movements. It has greatly magnified them. Again and again, exchange rates are determined by expectations of what they will be tomorrow, next month or next year. When markets come to see that exchange-rate stability is not itself an important policy objective, they induce snowballing movements widely out of keeping with current balance-of-payments prospects or domestic price movements. Swings in exchange rates have, in fact, proved large enough to damage the growth and stability both of countries with depreciating currencies and of those with appreciating currencies.

At the heart of these developments is the failure to realise that to function effectively the dollar, and any other leading currency with an international role, will continue to need a system of international support. In today's conditions unmanaged floating rates prove to be an expression of unilateralism and a rejection of international order in an area crucial to the well-being of everyone.

3. Trade Deficits

It was recognised after the war that the world needed a mechanism to mitigate the possibly injurious consequences of trading imbalances, not just for the sake of the country in difficulties but for all its trading partners. The IMF was therefore set up to help to regulate parities and to soften the tendency of payment imbalances producing unnecessary contraction in the deficit economies and harm to world trade. In practice the operations of the IMF are too limited and short term. More damagingly, they are focussed far too heavily on the problems of temporary deficit of advanced countries. The credit facilities of the IMF were never related to financing longer-term deficits of developing countries or those whose rhythm of imbalance was more prolonged than conventional wisdom allowed.

After the war there developed a consensus that the poorer countries should receive a continuing net transfer of resources. Again, there was insufficient intellectual clarity. It was never certain whether the advanced countries were engaged in an act of enlightened modern philanthropy or were advancing global political and economic causes. There were no principles, only a rather arbitrary set of arrangements for soft loans and grants brought into being by governments, sometimes giving money directly and sometimes indirectly through institutions such as the World Bank. Money was not spent as effectively as it might have been.

Still, the system limped along. There was a balance of benefit. It was not until OPEC suddenly quadrupled the price of oil that the underlying confusion was dramatically revealed. In the 1960s the arrangements for deficit financing never caused serious financial crisis. The worst result was protracted negotiations between the bureaucrats of the debtor and creditor countries. The accountancy which prevails in relations between governments, whatever other disturbing features it may have, did not threaten the bankruptcy of either the lending or borrowing governments or the viability of the world banking system.

The OPEC price rise changed that landscape – and we are still stumbling blindly in its savage contours. The rise imposed on developing countries a catastrophic increase in the finance required to meet their imbalances. Only with the greatest difficulty could the big developed countries find the money to lend the debtors. The private banking system was enlisted to fill the gap. It recycled the huge OPEC deposits. It did this in an atmosphere of false optimism and unjustified self-congratulation by everyone concerned. The very dangerous consequences to the solvency of the banks and the debtor countries have been discussed in full in Chapters 3 and 4.

Throughout this dismal catalogue there is a common theme. The leaders of the world, whether they be politicians, civil servants or central bankers, have consistently failed to provide strategic thinking. Matters are handled piecemeal with no sense of overall design. The case-by-case approach, justified from one angle, is elevated to high principle. In reality, it is a sign of intellectual bankruptcy, a euphemism for abdicating responsibility for the aggregate result of our actions. 'Leave it to the market', we are told, as if financial markets operate in a vacuum and are not powerfully conditioned by the actions of our great institutions.

H. L.

ACKNOWLEDGEMENTS

Seek not to present a perfect work.
THE LADY JULIAN OF NORWICH

An apology is required from anyone adding to the pile of literature on the world crisis of debt and growth, which has mounted as exponentially as the debts to which it refers.

In this short analysis we have set out to write a lucid description of the problem which clearly distinguishes the wood from the trees, which is uninfluenced by the need to play out any active role in the unfolding drama and which is accessible to the lay reader without abandoning some of the subtleties of interest to the student of the subject. We are only too aware, after several slipped deadlines, that it is a tall order.

There are a number of people we would like to thank for their help. Peter Mayer and Andrew Franklin of Penguin Books have both been exasperated and enthusiastic in tactful measure. Our research assistant Brigitte Adès provided unstinting support and was of particular help with the passages on the history of defaults in the 1930s and before and on the relationship between armaments and the debt build-up. Dr Vince Cable, Professor Rudiger Dornbusch and Peter Rodgers helped with useful conversations. Many others also assisted us during our research, but their careers in banking of government would not benefit from acknowledgement. We thank them nevertheless. Betty Payton, Stephanie Tewson and Barbara de Lord typed draft chapters with amazing speed and efficiency. Dr Ray Richardson provided many useful comments on our first draft, while Dr Stephany Griffith-Jones and Professor Susan Strange kindly read and commented helpfully on the second. Finally, we thank our wives, Diane and Vicky, who made time for us by shouldering more than their fair share of marital, domestic and parental duties and who provided essential support and encouragement. Whatever errors of fact or judgement this book may contain are indisputably ours.

Harold Lever
Christopher Huhne
London, 15 September 1985

NOTES

I INTRODUCTION AND SUMMARY

1 This figure is derived from IMF, *World Economic Outlook*, Washington DC, April 1985. See Chapter 2, Table 3.

2 THE STATE OF THE PROBLEM

1 Some useful history is provided by Carlos F. Diaz-Alejandro, 'Stories of the 1930s for the 1980s', in Pedro Aspe Armella *et al.* (eds.), *Financial Policies and the World Capital Market: The Problem of Latin American Countries*, University of Chicago Press, Chicago, 1983, pp. 5–35. See also William Wynne, *State Insolvency and Foreign Bondholders: Case Histories*, Vol. 2, Yale University Press, New Haven, 1951; Max Winkler, *Foreign Bonds: An Autopsy*, R. Swain & Co., Philadelphia, 1933; Clifford Dammers, 'A Brief History of Sovereign Defaults and Rescheduling', in David Suratgar (ed.), *Default and Rescheduling: Corporate and Sovereign Borrowers in Difficulty*, Euromoney Publications, London, 1984.

2 World Bank, *World Debt Tables 1984–5*, Washington DC, 1985, p. ix.

3 IMF, *World Economic Outlook*, Washington DC, April 1985, Tables 45 and 46, pp. 262–3.

4 Rudiger Dornbusch, 'The Debt Problem: 1980–84 and Beyond' (mimeo), MIT, Boston, January 1985, p. 4.

5 Federal Financial Institutions Examination Council, E.16 (126), Washington DC, October 1984; Board of Governors of the Federal Reserve System, Washington DC.

6 Federal Financial Institutions Examination Council, E.16 (126).

7 The UK banks' external liabilities in foreign currency amounted to $496 billion at the end of 1984, according to the BIS's figures in *International Banking Developments: Fourth Quarter, 1984*, Basle, April 1985. The UK Treasury valued its official foreign-currency reserves at $14.3 billion in June 1985 (press notice).

8 *Financial Times*, 21 May 1985.

9 BIS, *International Banking Developments: Fourth Quarter, 1984*.

10 IMF, *World Economic Outlook*, April 1985, p. 3.

11 See C. I. Brown, 'LDC Debts – the Accounting and Auditing Response', paper given at the Institute of Chartered Accountants in England and Wales Conference, 1984.

12 See IMF, *World Economic Outlook*, April 1985, Chapter III–1, p. 80.

13 UNECLA, *Balance preliminar de la Economia Latinoamericana en 1984*, Santiago de Chile, 1985, Cuadro 3.

14 The resource flow is computed from IMF data by taking the balance-of-payments current-account deficit – the deficit of payments of foreign exchange for imports, services and interest, profits and dividends – and deducting the payments included in that figure for interest, profits and dividends. Where interest, profits and dividend outflows are larger than the rest of the current-account deficit, the country concerned must be running a surplus of exports of goods and services over its imports and thereby transferring resources to its creditors. The figures in the table are a first approximation, since they do not include profits remitted on direct investment.

15 UNECLA, *Balance preliminar de la Economia Latinoamericana en 1984.*

16 Database of Data Resources, Inc.

17 Inter-American Development Bank, *Annual Report 1984*, Washington DC, 1985, Table 8, p. 123.

18 Mario-Henrique Simonsen, 'The Developing Country Debt Problem' (mimeo), paper for World Bank Conference, February 1984, in G. Smith and J. Cuddington (eds.), *International Debt and the Developing Countries*, World Bank, Washington DC, 1985.

19 IMF, *World Economic Outlook*, April 1985, p. 57.

20 UNCTAD, *Trade and Development Report 1984*, Geneva, 1984, pp. 35, 158.

21 *Financial Times*, 18 May 1985.

3 THE ORIGINS OF THE CRISIS I:
THE DEMAND FOR CREDIT

1 See, for example, M. Brzoska, 'The Military Related External Debt of Third World Countries', *Journal of Peace Research*, Vol. 20, No. 3, 1983; Walter F. Kitchenman, 'Arms Transfers and the Indebtedness of Less Developed Countries', N-2020-FF, Rand Corporation, Santa Monica, December 1983; GATT, *International Trade 1982–3*, Geneva, 1983; IMF, *World Economic Outlook*, Washington DC, May 1984, p. 63.

2 Ronald Leven and David L. Roberts, 'Latin America's Prospects for Recovery', *Federal Reserve Bank of New York Quarterly Review*, Vol. 8, No. 3, Autumn 1983, p. 7.

3 IMF, *International Financial Statistics Yearbook*, Washington DC, 1984.

4 See Edward R. Tufte, *Political Control of the Economy*, Princeton University Press, Princeton, 1978, Figure 3–1, p. 68.

5 See IMF, *International Financial Statistics Yearbook 1984*, and various issues of *World Economic Outlook* for subsequent figures in this section.

6 William R. Cline, *International Debt: Systemic Risk and Policy Response*, Institute for International Economics, Washington DC, 1984, Table 1.3, p. 10.

7 See Chapter 2, Table 3.

8 UNCTAD, *International Monetary Issues*, TD/B/C.3/194, Geneva, 1984, Table 3, p. 13. The figure refers to the excess debt incurred between 1980 and 1982 as a result of actual interest rates rather than those prevailing in 1976–9.

9 Inter-American Development Bank, *Annual Report 1984*, Washington DC, 1985, Table 12, p. 126.

10 IMF, *International Financial Statistics Yearbook 1984*, All Commodities Index, p. 133.

11 SIPRI, *Yearbook 1982*, Stockholm, 1983, Table 6.1, p. 177.

12 Michael Rich, William Stanley, John Birkler, Michael Hesse, 'Multinational Coproduction of Military Aerospace Systems', R-2861-AF, Rand Corporation, Santa Monica, October 1981, p. 73.

13 SIPRI, *Yearbook 1982*.

14 See Brzoska, 'The Military Related External Debt of Third World Countries'.

15 See Kitchenman, 'Arms Transfers and the Indebtedness of Less Developed Countries'.

16 Rudiger Dornbusch, 'The Debt Problem and Options for Debt Relief' (mimeo), MIT, Boston, September 1984, Table 4, p. 7.

17 Carlos F. Diaz-Alejandro, 'Latin American Debt: I Don't Think We Are in Kansas Any More', *Brookings Papers on Economic Activity*, 2, 1984, Table 1, p. 342. This paper gives a very useful table of real exchange rates in Latin America over time, on which we draw heavily in this passage.

18 Jeffrey Sachs's comment on Diaz-Alejandro, 'Latin-American Debt', in *Brookings Papers on Economic Activity*, 2, 1984, p. 397.

4 THE ORIGINS OF THE CRISIS 2:
THE SUPPLY OF CREDIT

1 OECD, *The Internationalization of Banking: The Policy Issues*, Paris, 1983; BIS, *International Banking Developments: Fourth Quarter 1984*, Basle, 1985.

2 OECD, *The Internationalization of Banking*; BIS, *International Banking Developments: Fourth Quarter, 1984*, p. 2.

3 Anthony Sampson, *The Money Lenders*, Hodder & Stoughton, London, 1981, p. 127.

4 Press release.

5 Clifford Dammers, 'A Brief History of Sovereign Defaults and Rescheduling', in David Suratgar (ed.), *Default and Rescheduling: Corporate and Sovereign Borrowers in Difficulty*, Euromoney Publications, London, 1984, p. 77.

6 *IMF Survey*, May 1974, quoted in D. Lomax, *The Developing Country Debt Crisis* (forthcoming).

7 Press releases.

8 Communiqué published in the *Financial Times*, 30 June 1979.

9 'The Recycling Problem Revisited', *Challenge*, Vol. 23, July–August 1980, p. 13 (quoted in *Brookings Papers on Economic Activity*, 2, 1984).

10 Roland Plan, 'External Debt Rescheduling: Repercussions on and Attitudes of the Lending Banks' (mimeo), Institut d'Administration et de Gestion, Université Catholique de Louvain, Louvain, 1984.

11 R. W. Lombardi, *Debt Trap: Rethinking the Logic of Development*, Praeger, New York, 1985, p. 106.

12 BIS, *International Banking Developments: Fourth Quarter, 1984*.

13 William R. Cline, *International Debt: Systemic Risk and Policy Response*, Institute for International Economics, Washington DC, 1984, p. 113.

14 Hyman P. Minsky, 'The Financial Instability Hypothesis: a Restatement' (mimeo), Centro Studi di Confederazione Generale dell' Industria Italiana, January 1979.

15 IMF, *World Economic Outlook*, Washington DC, June 1981, Table 2, p. 112.

16 Cline, *International Debt*, Table 1.1, p. 2.

17 'Overview Paper on Debt' (mimeo), background papers for the Commonwealth expert group on debt, CDG/1/ComSec, April 1984.

5 A CRITIQUE OF THE IMF'S 'SOLUTION'

1 Jacques de Larosière, speech to the International Monetary Conference, Philadelphia, 4 June 1984, in *IMF Survey*, 18 June 1984.

2 Jacques de Larosière, speech to a symposium organized by the Federation of Swedish Industries, Stockholm, 6 February 1985 (IMF press release).

3 IMF, *International Financial Statistics*, Washington DC, February 1985, p. 71.

4 The IMF seemed rather less certain of this process in 1985 than it had been the year before. In 1985 it said that developments along the lines of its 'baseline scenario' would 'at least open the door to a gradual renewal of growth in capital flows to the developing countries' (IMF, *World Economic Outlook*, Washington DC, April 1985, p. 192). In 1984 it had said, referring particularly to the hump of repayments of debt coming due in 1987: 'It should be possible to manage the bulk of the financing requirements by means of spontaneous refinancing of the credits being amortized' (IMF, *World Economic Outlook*, Washington DC, May 1984, p. 70).

5 Professor William Cline, whose views are similar to those of the IMF, puts the theory well: 'The large adjustment made in 1983 meant that for 1984 and beyond the principal need was not for further increases in trade balances but rather for a parallel rise in

both exports and imports, so that higher import levels compatible with the reactivation of growth would be available without recourse to foreign borrowing', *International Debt: Systemic Risk and Policy Response*, Institute for International Economics, Washington D C, 1984, p. 154.

6 Rudiger Dornbusch, 'The Debt Problem: 1980–84 and Beyond' (mimeo), M I T, Boston, 1985, p. 17.

7 Inter-American Development Bank, *External Debt and Economic Development in Latin America*, Washington D C, January 1984, pp. 45 and 63 and Table A.1.05, p. 75.

8 U N E C L A, *Balance preliminar de la Economia Latinoamericana en 1984*, Santiago de Chile, 1985, Cuadro 4.

9 ibid., Cuadro 1.

10 Anatole Kaletsky, *The Costs of Default*, a Twentieth Century Fund Paper, Priority Press Publications, New York, 1985.

11 W. Greenwell and Co., *Banking Commentary*, London, May 1985.

12 See, for example, U S Secretary of State George Shultz's speech at Princeton, 12 April 1985: 'There is no escaping this hard conclusion: domestic saving and private foreign equity investment will be the main sources of funds available to finance development and stimulate growth.' Domestic saving, of course, cannot finance deficits on the current account of the balance of payments, which are in foreign currency.

13 Derived from I M F, *World Economic Outlook*, Washington D C, April 1985, Table 40, p. 254.

14 I M F, *World Economic Outlook*, Occasional Paper 32, Washington D C, September 1984, Table 27, p. 59.

15 I M F, *World Economic Outlook*, April 1985, p. 193.

16 ibid.

6 ECONOMIC UNCERTAINTIES AND THE GROWTH OF PROTECTIONISM

1 I M F, *World Economic Outlook*, Washington D C, April 1985, Table 50, p. 271ff.

2 O E C D, *Economic Outlook*, Paris, December 1984, Table 7, p. 43.

3 I M F, *World Economic Outlook*, Occasional Paper 27, Washington D C, May 1984, Table 49, p. 221.

4 See Phil Suttle's critique of Cline and others, 'Debt Projection Models: a Survey and Comparison' (mimeo), International Division of the Bank of England, London, February 1985.

5 I M F, *World Economic Outlook*, Occasional Paper 32, Washington D C, September 1984, Table II, p. 12.

6 William R. Cline, *International Debt: Systemic Risk and Policy Response*, Institute for International Economics, Washington D C, 1984.

7 Morgan Guaranty, *World Financial Markets*, New York, various issues (particularly October/November 1984).

8 Cline, *International Debt*, Table 7.1, p. 127.

9 For a comparison of the methods and results of various debt-projection models see Suttle, 'Debt Projection Models'. He concludes that the studies 'do not give unambiguous opinion-free answers since their conclusions are based ultimately on the interpretation of a set of data by the author who, for example, has no set of statistical tables to use to test his null hypothesis. Thus, they tend to be used to provide supposed empirical evidence to back up the author's existing views on the likely outcome of the debt crisis.'

10 Figures in UNECLA, *Balance preliminar de la Economia Latinoamericana en 1984*, Santiago de Chile, 1984.

11 Speech by Jacques de Larosière, Philadelphia, 4 June 1984, quoted in *IMF Survey*, 18 June 1984.

12 Professor Cline, for example, appears to assume that non-oil imports have a one-for-one relationship whereby a 1 per cent trend growth causes a 1 per cent import growth, though the short-run cyclical response is a 3 per cent import rise for a 1 per cent rise in GDP: Cline, *International Debt*, p. 43.

13 Morgan Guaranty, *World Financial Markets*, New York, October/November 1984, Table 10, p. 8.

14 UNCTAD, *Trade and Development Report 1984*, Vol. II, Geneva, July 1984, Part II, p. 20. The report contains an excellent overview of the erosion of GATT, together with an annex estimating levels and costs of non-tariff protection.

15 Cline, *International Debt*, p. 198.

16 Carlos F. Diaz-Alejandro, 'Latin American Debt: I Don't Think We Are in Kansas Any More, *Brookings Papers on Economic Activity*, 2, 1984, p. 354.

17 See, for example, Jan Tumlir in *Economic Impact*, No. 48, Washington DC, 1984. Other estimates include 60 per cent under restraint in 1980 (François David of the French Ministry of Trade) and 48 per cent (Sheila Page, then of the National Institute of Economic and Social Research, now of the Overseas Development Institute, London).

18 Banco de Mexico.

19 Cline, *International Debt*, p. 197.

20 UNCTAD, *Trade and Development Report 1984*, p. 37.

21 Cline, *International Debt*, p. 198.

22 'US–Mexico export subsidy pact', *Financial Times*, 25 April 1985.

23 IMF, *World Economic Outlook*, September 1984, p. 12.

24 League of Nations, *World Economic Survey*, Geneva, 1932, pp. 165, 166.

7 THE POLITICAL ECONOMY OF DEFAULT

1 Inter-American Development Bank figures as a proportion of the World Bank's estimates of the total for 1982, or Data Resources, Inc.'s estimates as a proportion of World Bank estimates for 1984. Private debt figures from BIS, *International Banking Developments: Fourth Quarter, 1984*, Basle, April 1985.

2 *Business Week*, 27 May 1985 and 12 August 1985; *Economist*, 17 August 1985.

3 OECD-BIS, *Statistics on External Indebtedness at End December 1984*, Paris and Basle, July 1985.

4 Quoted in the *Report of the National Bipartisan Commission on Central America*, chaired by former Secretary of State Dr Henry Kissinger, Washington DC, 1984, Chapter 4, p. 41.

5 *Financial Times*, 15 November 1983.

6 *International Herald Tribune*, October 1983.

7 *Guardian*, 3 June 1985, and *The Times*, 4 June 1985.

8 *Guardian*, 15 July 1983.

9 *International Herald Tribune*, March 1984, and *The Times*, 25 January 1983.

10 *International Herald Tribune*, March 1985.

11 *The Times*, 20 February 1985.

12 *Daily Telegraph*, 3 June 1985.

13 *International Herald Tribune*, 10 October 1983.

14 *Business Week*, 12 August 1985.

15 For sources see Table 10.

16 For a discussion see, for example, Mark Gersovitz, 'Banks' International Lending Decisions: What Do We Know? Implications for Future Research', in G. Smith and J. Cuddington (eds.), *International Debt and the Developing Countries*, World Bank, Washington DC, 1985.

17 American Express International Banking Corporation, *Amex Bank Review*, Special Papers No. 10 and first and second supplements, London, March 1984, pp. 166, 167.

18 World Bank, *World Debt Tables 1984–5*, Washington DC, 1985; BIS, *International Banking Developments: Fourth Quarter, 1984*.

19 OECD-BIS, *Statistics on External Indebtedness at End December 1984*.

20 R. T. McNamar to the International Forum of the United States Chamber of Commerce, Washington DC, 12 October 1983, quoted in R. Dornbusch, 'On Muddling through the Debt Crisis', *World Economy*, Vol. 7, Trade Policy Research Centre, London, June 1984, part 2, p. 148.

21 The best discussion known to us of the costs and benefits of default, on which these paragraphs draw heavily, is Anatole Kaletsky, *The*

Costs of Default, a Twentieth Century Fund Paper, Priority Press Publications, New York, 1985.

22 *Allied Bank* v. *Banco Credito Agricola de Cartago*, 1983, quoted in ibid., p. 24.

23 Quoted in full in ibid., p. 86.

24 Georges R. Delaume, 'Special Risk and Remedies of International Sovereign Loans', in David Suratgar (ed.), *Default and Rescheduling: Corporate and Sovereign Borrowers in Difficulty*, Euromoney Publications, London, 1984, p. 103.

25 For a discussion see Robin Renwick, 'Economic Sanctions', Centre for International Affairs, Harvard University, 1981; M. S. Daoudi and M. S. Dajani, *Economic Sanctions: Ideals and Experience*, Routledge & Kegan Paul, London, 1983.

26 See Carlos F. Diaz-Alejandro, 'Stories of the 1930s for the 1980s', in Pedro Aspe Armella *et al.* (eds.), *Financial Policies and the World Capital Market: The Problem of Latin American Countries*, University of Chicago Press, Chicago, 1983, p. 29.

27 Thomas O. Enders and Richard P. Mattione, 'Latin America: the Crisis of Debt and Growth', *Studies in International Economics*, Brookings Institution, Washington DC, 1984.

28 *The Times*, 25 March 1983.

29 *Guardian*, 1 May 1985.

30 *Guardian*, 19 August 1985.

8 THE RISKS AND COSTS OF DOING NOTHING

1 Statement of the Hon. Donald T. Regan, Secretary of the Treasury, before the House Banking, Finance and Urban Affairs Committee, Washington DC, 21 December 1982.

2 William R. Cline, *International Debt: Systemic Risk and Policy Response*, Institute for International Economics, Washington DC, 1984, pp. 27, 28.

3 *Business Week*, 1 April 1985.

4 Cline, *International Debt*, p. 29.

5 See broker's analysis, James Capel & Co., London, 5 June 1984.

6 For an excellent discussion of international lenders of last resort see Stephany Griffith-Jones and Michael Lipton, 'International Lenders of Last Resort: Are Changes Required?', *Occasional Papers in International Trade and Finance*, Midland Bank International, London, March 1984.

7 BIS, *International Banking Developments: Fourth Quarter, 1984*, Basle, April 1985; UK Treasury press release.

8 *Bank of England Quarterly Bulletin*, Vol. 21, No. 2, June 1981, p. 238.

9 Data Resources, Inc., *US Review*, Lexington, Massachusetts, September 1983 and April 1984; Wharton Econometric Forecasting

Associates, 'What if Latin America Defaults?', Philadelphia, Fall 1984.

10 Sanjay Dhar in *Federal Reserve Bank of New York Quarterly Review*, Vol. 8, No. 3, Autumn 1983.

11 BIS *International Banking Developments: First Quarter, 1985*, Basle, July 1985.

9 TOWARDS REFORM

1 In our discussion of proposals we draw heavily on a useful and comprehensive survey of reform plans by Dr Stephany Griffith-Jones: 'Proposals to Manage Debt Problems: Review and Suggestions for Further Research' (mimeo), Institute of Development Studies, University of Sussex, 1985.

2 For a summary of some of these American proposals see William R. Cline, *International Debt: Systemic Risk and Policy Response*, Institute for International Economics, Washington DC, 1984, pp. 130–32.

3 See a description in Mario-Henrique Simonsen, 'The Developing Country Debt Problem' (mimeo), paper for World Bank Conference, February 1984, in G. Smith and J. Cuddington (eds.), *International Debt and the Developing Countries*, World Bank, Washington DC, 1985. Simonsen also points out that the proposal that the debtors should give their creditors foreign-exchange-earning assets – i.e. equity instead of debt – suffers from the flaw that it would reduce available foreign-exchange earnings as surely as do negative debt transfers. It therefore provides the debtors with no solution.